Series / Number 07-019

DISCRIMINANT ANALYSIS

WILLIAM R. KLECKA
University of Cincinnati

SAGE PUBLICATIONS / Beverly Hills / London

Christopher J. Carlini

For information address:

SAGE Publications, Inc.   SAGE Publications Ltd
275 South Beverly Drive 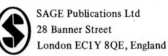 28 Banner Street
Beverly Hills, California 90212   London EC1Y 8QE, England

International Standard Book Number 0-8039-1491-1

Library of Congress Catalog Card No. L. C. 80-50927

FIRST PRINTING

When citing a professional paper, please use the proper form. Remember to cite the
correct Sage University Paper series title and include the paper number. One of the
two following formats can be adapted (depending on the style manual used):

(1) IVERSEN, GUDMUND R. and NORPOTH, HELMUT (1976) "Analysis of Variance." Sage University Paper series on Quantitative Applications in the Social
Sciences, 07-001. Beverly Hills and London: Sage Pubns.

OR

(2) Iversen, Gudmund R. and Norpoth, Helmut. 1976. *Analysis of Variance*. Sage
University Paper series Quantitative Applications in the Social Sciences, series no.
07-001. Beverly Hills and London: Sage Publications.

CONTENTS

Editor's Introduction 5

1. Background 7
   When To Use Discriminant Analysis—the Basic
      Assumptions 8
   Some Social Science Examples 12
   Additional Readings 14

2. Deriving the Canonical Discriminant Functions 15
   A Spatial Interpretation 16
   The Number of Canonical Discriminant Functions 16
   Deriving the Canonical Discriminant Function
      Coefficients 18
   Raw Coefficients 22
   Unstandardized Coefficients 22

3. Interpreting the Canonical Discriminant Functions 23
   Calculating Discriminant Scores 24
   Two-Function Plots 27
   One-Function Plots 28
   Standardized Coefficients 29
   Structure Coefficients 31
   How Many Functions are Significant? 34
      The Number of Functions 34
      The Relative Percentage 35
      The Canonical Correlation 36
      Measuring Residual Discrimination with
         Wilks's Lambda 38
      Testing the Significance of Wilks's Lambda 40

4. Classification Procedures 42
   Classification Functions 42
      Simple Classification Functions 43
      Generalized Distance Functions 44
      Probability of Group Membership 45
   Adjusting for Prior Probabilities or Cost of
   Misclassification 46

Classification Based on Canonical Discriminant
    Functions 47
Territorial Plots 49
The Classification Matrix 49
Split-Sample Validation 51

5. Stepwise Inclusion of Variables 52
    Selection Criteria 54
        Wilks's Lambda and the Partial F Ratio 54
        Rao's V 54
        Mahalanobis Squared Distance Between
            Closest Groups 55
        Between-Groups F 55
        Minimizing Residual Variance 56
    Minimum Conditions for Selection 56
        Tolerance 57
        F-To-Enter 57
        F-To-Remove 57
    A Stepwise Example 58

6. Concluding Remarks 60
    Violation of Assumptions 60
    Other Problems 63
    In Conclusion 63

Notes 65

References 69

Editor's Introduction

In DISCRIMINANT ANALYSIS, William Klecka presents a lucid and simple introduction to several related statistical procedures known as discriminant analysis. His treatment is practical with many helpful applications and examples throughout. In the first chapter, Klecka nicely covers the basic assumptions of discriminant analysis, including both a verbal and a mathematical statement of these assumptions. In addition, he begins his treatment of the topic with several social science examples. Discriminant analysis provides a powerful technique for examining differences between two or more groups of objects with respect to several variables simultaneously. This technique has therefore been used successfully by, for example:

- psychologists studying personnel and educational testing—discriminant techniques are especially helpful in predicting (or explaining) which students will be successful, based on their differences on several variables, prior to admission to a particular educational program

- political scientists who examine voting behavior among citizens or among legislators—they attempt to isolate variables which discriminate among citizens who will vote for Democrats versus Republicans, for example, or among legislators who generally vote liberal versus conservative

- sociologists and psychologists who study sex-role behavior in children

- political scientists who study court case dispositions.

Many more examples, across many fields of social science, could be enumerated. The class of techniques labelled "discriminant analysis" is broadly useful and has been applied to a wide variety of research and predictive problems. Professor Klecka's introductory treatment of the topic is a very good place to begin. Students with little background will have no difficulty following his presentation, and he provides suggestions of more advanced treatments of the topic which will be comprehensible to the readers after they have mastered Klecka's material.

DISCRIMINANT ANALYSIS introduces canonical discriminant functions, classification functions and procedures, and various selection criteria for the inclusion of variables in discriminant analysis. Professor Klecka derives canonical discriminant function coefficients, provides a spatial interpretation of them, and provides a nice discussion of the interpretation of canonical discriminant functions. He presents a clear discussion of unstandardized and standardized coefficients, as well as procedures to determine how many discriminant functions are significant. Throughout the presentation, Professor Klecka is careful to begin as simply as possible and to build to a more complex understanding of the uses and abuses of discriminant analysis. At the end of his presentation, he has a discussion of the violation of the assumptions which underlie discriminant analysis. This discussion serves as an important guide for the novice who hopes to use discriminant analysis for the first time in a research problem. The discriminating consumer will readily recognize the quality of DISCRIMINANT ANALYSIS.

—John L. Sullivan, Series Editor

1. BACKGROUND

Discriminant analysis is a statistical technique which allows the researcher to study the differences between two or more groups of objects with respect to several variables simultaneously. In the social sciences, there are a wide variety of situations in which this technique may be useful. Consider, for example, a research team that has been commissioned to study the outcomes of terrorist take-overs involving hostages. In particular, they want to know what elements of the situation would predict the safe release of hostages even though the terrorists' demands have not been met. They hypothesize that several variables may be good predictors of safe release versus injury to or execution of the hostages. Among these variables are: the number of terrorists, the strength of their support in the local population, whether they are an independent group or members of a larger militant organization, the tone of their rhetoric, type and quantity of weapons, ratio of terrorists to hostage, and so on. By examining previous incidents in which authorities have refused to meet the terrorists' demands, the researchers hope to determine: (1) which, if any, of those variables are useful in predicting the ultimate fate of the hostages; (2) how these variables might be combined into a mathematical equation to predict the most likely outcome; and (3) the accuracy of the derived equation. Discriminant analysis can provide the necessary evidence. If past incidents of safe release of hostages do differ on the variables being studied from those in which the hostages were injured, then the prediction

AUTHOR'S NOTE: *I wish to thank Kenneth Janda for stimulating my interest in this topic and the following individuals for their many helpful comments on this paper: Lawrence Mayer, John Sullivan, Eric Uslaner, and Ronald Weber.*

equation would be helpful to authorities who deal with this type of terrorist activity.

Other areas in which this technique has been profitably employed include personnel placement testing, roll call analyses of legislatures, psychological testing of children, the effects of medical treatments, economic differences between geographic regions, predicting voting behavior, and many more. The basic prerequisites are that two or more groups exist which we presume differ on several variables and that those variables can be measured at the interval or ratio level.[1] Discriminant analysis will then help us analyze the differences between the groups and/or provide us with a means to assign (classify) any case into the group which it most closely resembles.

The remainder of this chapter will present more background information on what discriminant analysis is and when to use it. Subsequent chapters will deal with the task of interpreting the several statistics produced in the course of a discriminant analysis.

When To Use Discriminant Analysis—the Basic Assumptions

First of all, the *data cases* should be members of two or more mutually exclusive *groups*. Data cases are the basic units of analysis—the elemental things being studied. These may be people, animals, countries, the economy at different points in time, or whatever. In the terrorist example, each previous terrorist episode is a case. The groups must be defined so that each case belongs to one, and only one, group. The terrorist episodes are divided into two groups: those involving the safe release of all hostages versus those in which some or all hostages were killed or injured.

In some research settings, we may also have some cases which are not identified as belonging to any of the groups under analysis. This would include some number of cases whose group membership cannot be identified. Or, perhaps we are withholding them from the analysis for some reason. These are cases which will be classified into a group *later* on the basis of mathematical equations derived from an analysis of the cases with "known" memberships. In the terrorist example, one objective is to accurately predict the outcome of future incidents. Thus, future incidents can be considered as "ungrouped" or "unclassified" cases.

"Discriminant analysis" is a broad term which refers to several closely related statistical activities. In a given research situation, the analyst may not use all of them. For the sake of simplifying this presentation, I will divide these activities into those used for interpreting the group differences and those employed to classify cases into the groups. A researcher is

engaged in *interpretation* when studying the ways in which groups differ—
that is, is one able to "discriminate" between the groups on the basis of
some set of characteristics, how well do they discriminate, and which
characteristics are the most powerful discriminators? The other application is to derive one or more mathematical equations for the purpose of
classification. These equations, called "discriminant functions," combine
the group characteristics in a way that will allow one to identify the group
which a case most closely resembles. For instance, if the characteristics
of a new terrorist take-over most closely resemble those past incidents in
which the hostages were released without harm, the discriminant function
would indicate that this incident has a higher probability of being that
type as opposed to one in which hostages are harmed. (After the incident
is over, one knows whether the prediction was correct, but in many other
applications the researcher is not able to confirm the accuracy of the
classifications.) Frequently, of course, researchers use discriminant analysis for both interpretation and classification.

The characteristics used to distinguish among the groups are called
"discriminating variables." These variables must be measured at the
interval or ratio level of measurement, so that means and variances can
be calculated and so that they can be legitimately employed in mathematical equations. In the terrorism example, seven discriminating variables were mentioned (number of terrorists, strength of support, number
of weapons, and so on). In general, there is no limit on the number of
discriminating variables as long as the total number of cases exceeds the
number of variables by more than two.

There are, however, some limits on the statistical properties which the
discriminating variables are allowed to have. For one thing, no variable
may be a linear combination of other discriminating variables. A "linear
combination" is the sum of one or more variables which may have been
weighted by constant terms. Thus, one may not use either the sum or the
average of several variables along with all those variables. Likewise,
two variables which are perfectly correlated cannot be used at the same
time. This prohibition against linear combinations is the result of certain
mathematical requirements of the technique, but it also makes sense
intuitively. The variable defined by the linear combination does not
contain any new information beyond what is contained in the components,
so it is redundant.

Another assumption required for many applications is that the population covariance matrices are equal for each group.[2] The easiest and most
commonly used form of discriminant analysis employs a "linear" discriminant function, which is a simple linear combination of the discriminating variables. This method is the easiest, because the assumption of

equal group covariance matrices allows a simplification of the formulas used to calculate the discriminant function and certain tests of significance.

A further assumption is that each group is drawn from a population which has a multivariate normal distribution. Such a distribution exists when each variable has a normal distribution about fixed values on all the others (Blalock, 1979: 452). This permits the precise computation of tests of significance and probabilities of group membership. When this assumption is violated, the computed probabilities are not exact, but they may still be quite useful if interpreted with caution (Lachenbruch, 1975: 41-46).

These assumptions constitute the mathematical model on which the most common approaches to discriminant analysis rest. If the data for a particular problem do not satisfy the assumptions, the statistical results will not be a precise reflection of reality. The problem of violating assumptions will be discussed further in Chapter 6.

From the discussion, so far, it should be clear that discriminant analysis is used to study the differences between two or more groups and a set of discriminating variables. This relationship is shown in Figure 1. By con-

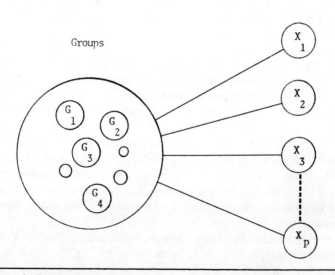

Figure 1: Relationship between groups and discriminating variables.

sidering the groups to be defined as a single nominal level variable (with each value denoting a different group), we see discriminant analysis as a technique which relates one nominal level variable to several interval level variables.

Notice that no mention has been made of the direction of causation and arrowheads were not used in Figure 1. The groups have not been defined as either the dependent or independent variable, and the same applies to the discriminating variables. If a research situation defines the group categories as dependent upon the discriminating variables, then that situation is analogous to the technique known as multiple regression. The primary difference is that discriminant analysis treats the dependent variable as being measured at the nominal level (i.e., groups). The earlier example of terrorist incidents was of this type. But when the values on the discriminating variables are defined as dependent upon the groups, discriminant analysis becomes an extension of multivariate analysis of variance. This situation typically arises from experimental settings, in which the group assignment is hypothesized to cause differences in several variables simultaneously.

Before leaving this background discussion, let me summarize the mathematical requirements which underlie discriminant analysis. In the way of notation, I shall use:

g = number of groups
p = number of discriminating variables
n_i = number of cases in group i
$n.$ = total number of cases over all the groups

The assumptions can be stated as:

(1) two or more groups: $g \geqslant 2$
(2) at least two cases per group: $n_i \geqslant 2$
(3) any number of discriminating variables, provided that it is less than the total number of cases minus two: $0 < p < (n. - 2)$
(4) discriminating variables are measured at the interval level
(5) no discriminating variable may be a linear combination of other discriminating variables
(6) the covariance matrices for each group must be (approximately) equal, unless special formulas are used
(7) each group has been drawn from a population with a multivariate normal distribution on the discriminating variables.

Some Social Science Examples

Researchers have used discriminant analysis in a wide variety of settings. It was first developed by Fisher (1936), who was seeking to solve problems in physical anthropology and biology. In the social sciences, some of the first applications dealt with psychological and educational testing (Tatsuoka and Tiedeman, 1954). Political scientists have found discriminant analysis to be useful in studying citizen voting behavior (Klecka, 1973), legislative factions (Kornberg and Frasure, 1971; Heyck and Klecka, 1973), and felony court case dispositions (Eisenstein and Jacob, 1977). Psychologists have made extensive use of discriminant analysis, especially in areas such as personnel and educational testing. The technique is especially useful, however, in analyzing experimental data when assignment to a "treatment" group is presumed to affect scores on several criterion variables. An example of this type is C. O. Klecka's (1974) study of sex-role stereotypes in children.

While space does not permit a detailed discussion of the examples mentioned above, I will develop one particular application as the central example in this paper. This example is taken from Bardes's (1975, 1976) analysis of senatorial factions on the issue of foreign aid during the period of 1953 to 1972. A brief overview follows and details will be presented as needed in the subsequent sections.

Bardes wanted to see how U.S. Senate voting factions changed over time, in particular, how stable they were from year to year and how much they were influenced by other issues. She knew that Senators were not simply divided into pro- and anti-foreign aid groups and that disagreements frequently transcended formal party affiliations. Arguments often broke out about the level of aid to be distributed, the form of aid (cash, goods, or loans), and whether the President or the Senate should take the initiative in this area. From reading the *Congressional Quarterly* accounts of debates and other substantive sources, Bardes was able to identify several factions and many of the Senators who adhered to them. Her problems were that the number of factions existing at any one time was not clear and that a large number of Senators did not identify their loyalties.

The solution she chose was a three-step statistical application repeated for each of the 10 sessions being studied. First, she selected the roll call votes that pertained to foreign policy legislation and used cluster analysis to reduce them to a limited number of scales. This tended to emphasize those votes on which there was greatest disagreement. In the second step all Senators who could be classified were assigned to issue-oriented factions. The number of groups generated was influenced by her substantive knowledge of senatorial alignments during that session. At this stage, Senators without clear issue positions were considered unclassified. Finally, she applied discriminant analysis to the voting scales to determine whether any groups should be combined for lack of meaningful differences in their patterns of voting behavior. The discriminant function equations were also used to classify the ambiguous Senators into the groups which most closely resembled their own patterns of voting. In addition, she was able to identify the issues which were most powerful in discriminating among the groups. By comparing the results over time, she charted the growth and decline of several factions and documented significant changes that were associated with the inauguration of new Presidents and the disruption of the Vietnam war.

For the examples to be used in this paper, we will be looking at Bardes's data from the 84th Senate (1955-1956).[3] Her procedure for identifying the factions yielded four factions in this period and 19 Senators who could be clearly assigned to these factions (these represent the "known" or "classified" cases). The factions (groups) were as follows:

Group	Number of Cases	Description
1	9	Generally favoring foreign aid
2	2	Generally opposing foreign aid
3	5	Opposed to foreign involvements
4	3	Anti-Communists

To obtain the discriminating variables, Bardes aggregated the relevant roll call votes for that period into the following six scales:

Scale	Description
CUTAID	Cut aid funds
RESTRICT	Add restrictions to the aid program
CUTASIAN	Cut funds for Asian nations
MIXED	Mixed issues: liberal aid vs. no aid to communists
ANTIYUGO	Anti-aid to Yugoslavia
ANTINEUT	Anti-aid to neutral countries

These scales were defined as the average vote on the roll calls concerning that issue. CUTAID, for example, was computed from 10 separate roll call votes. On each individual vote, a Senator was given a score of 1 if his vote reflected opposition to the general topic (i.e., opposing efforts to cut aid or favoring efforts to increase aid), a score of 2 if he abstained or was absent, and a score of 3 if his vote was favorable to the general topic (i.e., favoring efforts to cut aid or opposing efforts to increase aid). Table 1 shows the mean (average) scale value for each of the six variables broken down by the groups. As we would expect, group 1 (favor aid) generally voted against measures to cut foreign aid (mean on CUTAID = 1.422), while group 2 (oppose aid) had the highest average score (3.000); and the other two groups fell at intermediate positions. In general, the groups tend to have different scores on each scale,[4] so we would expect these variables to have at least some ability to discriminate among the factions. These univariate statistics, however, do not tell us much about the multivariate differences between the groups. As the presentation progresses, I will be using these data to illustrate how discriminant analysis provides evidence about the multivariate group differences and the classification of the remaining 81 Senators into the four factions.

Additional Readings

Tatsuoka and Tiedeman (1954) and Kendall (1968) provide interesting discussions of the historical development of discriminant analysis. The former work also cities many of the early applications of this technique in psychology, educational testing, and biometrics. Morrison's (1969, 1974) works provide a good summary of discriminant analysis with only a limited dependence on mathematical formulas. His latter piece also contains a review of instances in which discriminant analysis has been used by marketing researchers.

Several textbooks oriented to applied social statistics discuss this technique. Lachenbruch (1975), Cooley and Lohnes (1971), Overall and Klett (1972), Tatsuoka (1971), and Van de Geer (1971) each have a different perspective, but between them they cover the ground rather thoroughly. These texts do assume some knowledge of matrix algebra, but

TABLE 1
Means for "Known" Senators

| Variable | Group | | | | Total |
	1	2	3	4	
CUTAID	1.422	3.000	2.200	2.100	1.900
RESTRICT	1.944	1.000	2.000	2.333	1.921
CUTASIAN	1.000	3.000	2.000	1.333	1.526
MIXED	2.667	2.000	1.800	1.667	2.211
ANTIYUGO	1.556	2.500	2.600	3.000	2.158
ANTINEUT	1.259	1.667	2.133	2.444	1.719

their treatments do not require the mathematical sophistication needed for the "classics," such as Anderson (1958) and Rao (1952, 1965).

Anyone using this technique would be well-advised to read the manual for the computer program to be used for the analysis. At a minimum, it will list the features and limitations of the program (there is considerable variation). Sometimes a summary of the technique and relevant equations will be given along with bibliographic references. Among the more widely distributed computer packages, the chapter in the SPSS manual (Klecka, 1975) is the most thorough, although it avoids presenting mathematical formulas (see Norusis, 1979, for a complete list of formulas used by SPSS). The discussions in the BMD manual (Dixon, 1973) and the SAS manual (Barr et al., 1976) are only brief presentations of the program features without explanations on how to interpret the output.

Veldman (1967) and Cooley and Lohnes (1971) provide FORTRAN source listings for those who want to write their own programs. The state of the art has surpassed these volumes, however, so do-it-yourself programmers would be wise to build their programs from the newer packages of mathematical subroutines available at most computing facilities. The sample data and examples provided in these texts, however, can be used to test the homemade program.

2. DERIVING THE CANONICAL DISCRIMINANT FUNCTIONS

Before discussing the topic of classification (which is handled in Chapter 4), I shall deal with the use of canonical discriminant functions to study the nature of group differences. This chapter will cover the basic rationale behind the computation of the canonical discriminant functions and strategies for determining how many functions to use.

A canonical discriminant function is a linear combination of the discriminating variables which are formed to satisfy certain conditions. It has the following mathematical form:

$$f_{km} = u_0 + u_1 X_{1km} + u_2 X_{2km} + \ldots + u_p X_{pkm}, \qquad [1]$$

where f_{km} = the value (score) on the canonical discriminant function for case m in the group k;

X_{ikm} = the value on discriminating variable X_i for case m in group k; and

u_i = coefficients which produce the desired characteristics in the function.

We derive the coefficients (the u's) for the first function so that the group means on the function are as different as possible. (A precise definition of "maximum group differences" will be given later.) The coefficients for the second function are also derived to maximize the differences between the group means but under the added condition that values on the second function are not correlated with values on the first function. A third function can be defined in a similar fashion having coefficients which maximize group differences while being uncorrelated with the previous functions, and so forth. The maximum number of unique functions we can derive in this fashion is equal to the number of groups minus one or the number of discriminating variables, whichever is fewer. In the Senate roll call example, there are six variables but only four groups, so three functions are the most we can get.

A Spatial Interpretation

Let us consider the discriminating variables as axes that define a p-dimensional space. Each data case is a point in this space with coordinates that are the case's value on each of the variables. If the groups differ in their behavior with respect to these variables, we can imagine each group as being a swarm of points concentrated in some portion of this space. While the groups may overlap somewhat, their respective "territories" are not identical. To summarize the position of a group, we can compute its "centroid." A group centroid is an imaginary point which has coordinates that are the group's mean on each of the variables. In the roll call example, the Senators are located in a six-dimensional space (the six voting scales), and the columns of Table 1 are the values of the centroids for each of the four groups.

Because each centroid represents the typical position for its group, we can study them to obtain an understanding of how the groups differ. Examining the individual variables, however, keeps us at the univariate level; and when there are a large number of variables, this information may be too complex to comprehend. As it turns out, we do not need so many dimensions to completely represent the relative positions of the group centroids. At the most, we need one less dimension than the number of groups.

The Number of Canonical Discriminant Functions

We can understand the influence of the number of groups by considering a geometric analogy. In any space where the rules of Euclidean geometry apply, two points will define the location of a straight line. In general, three points define a plane, four points define a three-dimensional surface, and so on. The principle is that the points define a space (line, plane, and so on) which has one less dimension than the number of points.

While the centroids define the space, there are still an infinite number of places where we can locate the axes (the coordinate system). A convenient place for the origin, the point at which each axis has a value of zero, is the "grand centroid," which is the position where the total set of data cases has its mean on each of the axes. Around this origin there are an infinite number of orientations for the axes, provided they stay within the space. Now, if we place one of those axes at an angle such that the group means on the axis are separated more than they would be for any other angle, we would have an axis with a great deal of intuitive meaning. Assuming that more axes exist (i.e., there are more than two groups), we can locate the second axis so that it, too, provides maximum separation of the groups but within the constraints that it is perpendicular to the first axis and stays within the space. Other axes can be positioned in a similar fashion.

By locating the axes in this fashion, we have met the criteria for the canonical discriminant functions. Equation 1 defines the mathematical transformation from the p-dimensional space of discriminating variables to the q-dimensional space of canonical discriminant functions (where q represents the maximum number of functions). There would be a separate equation such as Equation 1 for each of the axes. For a given data case, the values of f_{km} for each of the functions would represent that case's coordinates in the space of canonical discriminant functions.

An exception to the geometric rule stated above occurs when one or more of the centroids does not define a new dimension. An example of this is when three points fall on the same straight line or when four points fall into a single plane. Rather than defining a new dimension, one point fits into the space defined by the other points. This type of situation can go even further with four points falling on a single line, for example. In discriminant analysis, the same thing can happen. As we will see shortly, the four Senate factions (groups) in Bardes's analysis can be described very well by two functions and possibly even just one. In research situations, the excess dimension does not usually disappear completely, due to sampling and measurement errors. One can test each dimension, though, to see if it is statistically significant. If it is not significant, it can be ignored, because it is not likely to contribute much of theoretical or practical importance. This test is described later in the chapter.

In the situation in which the number of discriminating variables, p, is less than the number of groups, the maximum number of functions, q, is equal to p. Here, we are not making a translation from a space of many dimensions into' a space of a few dimensions. Rather, we are just relocating the axes to meet intuitively appealing criteria.

Deriving the Canonical Discriminant Function Coefficients

In this section, I will cover the basic principles underlying the derivation of the coefficients for the canonical discriminant functions, the u's. A complete understanding of the mathematical derivation is, however, beyond the scope of this paper. Several multivariate statistics texts, such as Cooley and Lohnes (1971), cover the material quite well for those who are interested.

To begin with, we need some statistical method for measuring the degree of differences among the data cases. A table of group means and standard deviations is not sufficient, because it cannot report the interrelations among the variables. We can, however, use the matrix of total sums of squares and cross-products, T, which is a square symmetric matrix.[5] To understand where T comes from, let us define some symbols as follows:

g = number of groups

n_k = number of cases in group k

$n.$ = total number of cases over all groups

X_{ikm} = the value of variable i for case m in group k

$X_{ik.}$ = mean value of variable i for those cases in group k

$X_{i..}$ = mean value of variable i for all cases (grand or total mean).

Now,

$$t_{ij} = \sum_{k=1}^{g} \sum_{m=1}^{n_k} (X_{ikm} - X_{i..})(X_{jkm} - X_{j..}). \qquad [2]$$

The terms in parentheses are the amount by which the value of a particular case deviates from the grand mean on that variable. When i = j, the two terms are the same, and we are just squaring the deviation. Thus, each diagonal element is the sum of squared deviations from the grand mean. This indicates how spread out the cases are on a single variable. When $i \neq j$, we are getting the sum of a deviation on one variable multiplied by the deviation on the other. This is one way of measuring the correlation (covariation) between the two variables, because it indicates how well a large deviation on one variable corresponds to a large deviation on the other. By taking the entire matrix, we have a summary of how much the points are spread out around the total space defined by all the variables; this is known as the dispersion.

If we were to divide each element of T by (n.-1), we would get the total covariance matrix. Although much of the discriminant analysis computations use T rather than the covariance matrix, much of the statistical literature talks about the covariance matrix. Covariance matrices can also be calculated for each group when they are based only on the cases for that group.

For the purpose of getting a feel for how strongly any two variables are related, we can examine the correlation between them. The correlation coefficient is more useful for this purpose than the covariance, because it is standardized to vary between –1 and +1. One can easily convert the T matrix into a matrix of correlation coefficients by dividing each element by the square root of the product of the two diagonal elements falling in the same row and column. (The same results can be achieved from the covariance matrix, see Cooley and Lohnes, 1971: 40.) Table 2 reports the total correlations for the Bardes data. Clearly, several of the variables are highly correlated which means that a Senator's score on one scale can be predicted fairly well by knowing his score on the other scale in that pair.

If the group locations are indeed distinct (i.e., the centroids are not identical), then the degree of dispersion within the groups will be less than the total dispersion. This is measured by the matrix W, which is called the within-group sums of squares and crossproducts matrix. W is very much like T, except that the deviations are measured from the mean of the group to which the case belongs (as opposed to the grand mean). The elements of W are defined as:

$$w_{ij} = \sum_{k=1}^{g} \sum_{m=1}^{n_k} (X_{ikm} - X_{ik.}) (X_{jkm} - X_{jk.}). \qquad [3]$$

When the elements of W are divided by (n.-g), we get the within-groups covariance matrix; it is essentially a weighted average of the group covariance matrices.

We can easily convert either W or the within-groups covariance matrix into a within-groups correlation matrix by the same procedure described for the total correlation matrix. Each correlation coefficient is an estimate

TABLE 2
Total Correlation Matrix

	CUTAID	RESTRICT	CUTASIAN	MIXED	ANTIYUGO	ANTINEUT
CUTAID	1.000					
RESTRICT	.043	1.000				
CUTASIAN	.787	.054	1.000			
MIXED	−.732	−.435	−.677	1.000		
ANTIYUGO	.534	.470	.498	−.638	1.000	
ANTINEUT	.526	.625	.562	−.829	.776	1.000

of the strength of the relationship between the corresponding pair of variables *within the groups*. This will usually differ from the total correlation, which is influenced by the group differences. If we assume the data cases are drawn either from the same population or from group populations that have identical dispersion patterns, the within-groups correlations are a better estimate of the relationships between the variables than the total correlations are. Table 3 gives the within-groups correlation matrix for the roll call data. As one can see, many of these values differ from the corresponding values in Table 2. This reflects the effect of looking only within the groups rather than considering the total range of cases, which is influenced by the differences in the group centroids.

When there are no differences among the group centroids, all the elements of W will equal the corresponding elements of T (because $X_{ik.}$ always equals $X_{i..}$). If, however, the centroids are different, the elements of W will be smaller than the corresponding elements of T. We measure this difference by the matrix B, which is defined as B = T − W (i.e., $b_{ij} = t_{ij} − w_{ij}$). B is called the between-groups sums of squares and crossproducts matrix. The size of the elements of B relative to those in W gives us a measure of how distinct the groups are, as I will discuss later.

TABLE 3
Within-Groups Correlation Matrix

	CUTAID	RESTRICT	CUTASIAN	MIXED	ANTIYUGO	ANTINEUT
CUTAID	1.000					
RESTRICT	.234	1.000				
CUTASIAN	.692	.562	1.000			
MIXED	−.706	−.547	−.834	1.000		
ANTIYUGO	.364	.647	.386	−.411	1.000	
ANTINEUT	.469	.744	.785	−.748	.645	1.000

The matrices W and B contain all the basic information about the relationships within the groups and between them. Through the use of calculus and other mathematical operations, we can derive a function with the properties desired. First, we have to solve the simultaneous equations defined by:

$$\Sigma b_{1i}v_i = \lambda \Sigma w_{1i}v_i$$
$$\Sigma b_{2i}v_i = \lambda \Sigma w_{2i}v_i$$
$$\cdot \qquad \cdot$$
$$\cdot \qquad \cdot \qquad\qquad [4]$$
$$\cdot \qquad \cdot$$
$$\Sigma b_{pi}v_i = \lambda \Sigma w_{pi}v_i,$$

where λ (lambda) is a constant called the "eigenvalue" and the v's are a set of p coefficients. As defined earlier, the b's and w's are, respectively, the between and within-groups sums of squares and crossproducts. The b's and w's are known quantities calculated from the sample data. Our objective is to solve the simultaneous equations given by Equation 4 for the values of lambda and the v's. In order to obtain unique solutions, we also set the condition that the sum of the squared values of the v's must be equal to 1.0. There are a maximum of q unique, nontrivial solutions to these equations. Each solution, which yields its own lambda and set of v's, corresponds to one canonical discriminant function.

The v coefficients could be used as the coefficients for the desired discriminant function. A simple adjustment to the values, however, will give us coefficients that give the function more desirable properties. These latter coefficients are the u's from Equation 1, and they are defined as:

$$u_i = v_i \sqrt{n. - g} \quad \text{and} \quad u_0 = - \sum_{i=1}^{p} u_i X_{i..} \qquad [5]$$

By employing the u's, the values of the f's (called "discriminant scores") for the data cases will be in standard form. This means that the discriminant scores over all the cases will have a mean of zero and a within-groups standard deviation of one.[6] The discriminant score for a given case represents the position of that case along the continuum (axis) defined by that function.

Raw Coefficients

The solution to Equation 4 yields a set of coefficients for each function, the v's. These raw coefficients could be used as they are for the purpose of classification. However, they are totally uninterpretable as coefficients, and the scores they produce for the data cases have no intrinsic meaning. The reason for this is that the solution has no logical constraint upon the origin or metric units used for the discriminant space. Although the space is created to provide maximum separation between the groups, the groups could be located anywhere in the space. This is like saying baseball players can position themselves *anywhere* on the field provided they are in the proper positions *relative* to one another. In addition, the north-south distances could be of one magnitude while the east-west distances were of another. This might result in first base being 100 feet from home plate while second base was only 25 feet from first base.

Some computer programs print these raw coefficients, and they can be used for classification purposes (to be discussed in Chapter 4). We can, however, make them more useful to us by making adjustments as given in Equation 5.

Unstandardized Coefficients

The process of adjusting the coefficients changes neither the amount of discrimination nor the relative positions of the groups. What happens is that the axes are shifted into a more meaningful location by moving the origin of the discriminant function axes (the point at which all the discriminant function axes have a value of zero) to coincide with the grand centroid. The grand centroid is that point in space where all of the discriminating variables have their average values over all cases. It is the "center" position for all the points representing the data cases. This relocation is helpful, because when we look at a group centroid or an individual case, we can tell right off where it is located relative to the center of the system. In the baseball analogy, this is equivalent to saying that home plate will always be located in one particular corner of the field, and the other bases will be located in fixed directions from home plate. Once the players see this layout, they can go to their respective positions quickly and easily.

The usual adjustments to the coefficients cause another change, too. This concerns the units used for measuring distances. The adjusted coefficients produce discriminant scores which are measured in standard deviation units. This means each axis is stretched or shrunk such that the score for a case represents the number of standard deviations it is from the grand centroid.[7] By looking at the score for a particular case one can immediately tell its relative distance from the origin *and* whether this is a great or small distance for the size of this system. Thus, a score of –2.5 tells us the case is two and a half standard deviations in the negative direction from the center of that axis. Because very few cases are more than two standard deviations from the mean regardless of the shape of the distribution, we know this case is quite distant from the center. In the baseball example, the standardization of distances is equivalent to saying that the distances from one base to the next will all be equal and that exactly the same distances will apply from one field to the next.

The way in which we make the adjustments discussed here depends upon whether the coefficients are to be used with the original data values or standardized data values. When we apply them to the original data, we refer to the coefficients as "unstandardized" coefficients, because the *original* data have not been standardized. The letter u has been employed here to denote these coefficients, and Equation 5 shows how to convert the v's into u's. (Standardized coefficients will be discussed in a later section.) One would normally use the unstandardized coefficients to compute the discriminant scores.

This chapter has concentrated on the mathematical derivation of the canonical discriminant functions. The objectives have been to give precise definitions for several of the symbols used in this paper and to offer the mathematically inclined reader some background on the derivation of these statistics. Applied social researchers do not normally need to have a firm grasp of this material. Rather, they should concentrate on learning to use and interpret the canonical discriminant functions, which is the purpose of the next chapter.

3. INTERPRETING THE
CANONICAL DISCRIMINANT FUNCTIONS

Once we have derived the canonical discriminant functions, we can move to interpreting their meaning. We find this meaning by (1) examining the relative positions of the data cases and group centroids and (2) studying the relationships between the individual variables and the functions. When more than one function exists, we also ask whether all of them are needed. To make the following discussion more concrete, let us begin by examining some results from Bardes's roll call analysis.

24

Calculating Discriminant Scores

Table 4 gives the unstandardized coefficients for the three functions derived from Bardes's data. These functions define a three-dimensional space in which the Senators can be located. Function 1 defines one of the axes. If we think of a typical three-dimensional space, Function 1 would most logically be the horizontal axis. The rules for deriving Function 2 require it to be perpendicular to Function 1, so that it represents completely different information (i.e., the two functions are not correlated). It would be the vertical axis. The third function must be perpendicular to both of these.[8]

The coefficients are used to compute the position of the data cases in the discriminant space. The formula for the first function is:

$$f_{km} = 5.4243 + .8087\,X_{1km} + .7940\,X_{2km} - 4.6004\,X_{3km}$$

$$- .6957\,X_{4km} - 1.1114\,X_{5km} + 1.4387\,X_{6km}, \qquad [6]$$

where f_{km} denotes the discriminant scores for case m on function one and the X's represent the original values that case m from group k has on each of the six discriminating variables. The formulas for the other two functions are similar with the corresponding numbers substituted for the u's.

These formulas tell us that we compute the discriminant scores by taking the original value for a case on each variable and multiplying it by the coefficient for that variable; we then add these products along with the constant term. (The constant term is the adjustment for the means, so that the mean discriminant score will be zero over all the cases.)

TABLE 4
Unstandardized Discriminant Coefficients

Variable	Unstandardized Coefficient		
	Function 1	Function 2	Function 3
Constant (u_0)	5.4243	3.5685	−4.3773
CUTAID	.8078	−.5225	1.6209
RESTRICT	.7940	−1.1177	−.3339
CUTASIAN	−4.6004	−1.1228	−1.1431
MIXED	−.6957	−1.3160	1.1418
ANTIYUGO	−1.1114	1.1132	.3781
ANTINEUT	1.4387	1.0422	.2000

Now let us pursue the actual computation of discriminant scores for one of the Senators used in this example. Table 5 gives the results for Senator Aiken (R, Vt.). Under each function, Table 5 presents the unstandardized coefficients and Aiken's corresponding raw data value for that scale.[9] The product of these two numbers yields the contribution of that scale to Aiken's total score on the corresponding function. The sum of the contributions gives the discriminant scores. Because the discriminant scores are coordinates in the subspace defined by the discriminant functions, we can see that Aiken's position is (2.25, -3.22, -.90).

We can also say something about how typical Aiken is of the Senators being analyzed. The discriminant scores help us, because they are in standard deviation units. On the first function, Aiken is off in the positive direction. (In a later section, we will learn this means he favors spending more on foreign aid.) Aiken's position on the second function is at the extreme negative end (which represents fewer restrictions). And on the third function, he is located somewhat in the negative direction (antiinvolvement).

As a second example, we can look at Senator Bridges (R, N.H.) whose raw data scores are: 1.0, 2.5, 1.4, 2.0 3.0, and 3.0, respectively. These translate into the following positions along the three axes: 1.37, 2.51, and -1.17. Clearly, Bridges and Aiken are located in different parts of the discriminant space. Bridges is not as far out on Fucntion 1, he is located in the opposite direction on Function 2, and he is slightly further in the negative direction on Function 3.

The unstandardized coefficients represent the amount of change in a case's position on that function if its score on the corresponding variable changed by one unit. If we could imagine a Senator changing his voting behavior so that his score on CUTAID went from 1.0 to 2.0 (while everything else remained the same), he would end up with a position on Function 1 that is .8078 units further in the positive direction. Of course, Senators cannot change their past voting behavior, but we can use the unstandardized coefficients to tell us something about the differences between two Senators. Aiken and Bridges have the same score on CUTAID, but on ANTIYUGO Aiken has a 1.0 while Bridges has a 3.0. This difference of two units means that ANTIYUGO causes Bridges to be 2.2228 units away from Aiken in the negative direction on Function 1 ($2 \times -1.1114 = -2.2228$). Because these Senators differ on other variables, too, we need to consider all of them before we know the net difference, but we are often interested in examining the impact of single variables while keeping all the others fixed.

In general, we do not get much from a case-by-case inspection of the data unless there are only a small number of cases. Our interest will usually

TABLE 5
Computation of Discriminant Scores for Senator Aiken

Variable	FUNCTION 1			FUNCTION 2			FUNCTION 3		
	Coeff.	× Value	= Contribution	Coeff.	× Value	= Contribution	Coeff.	× Value	= Contribution
Constant			5.4243			3.5685			-4.3773
CUTAID	.8078	1.0	.8078	-.5225	1.0	-.5225	1.6209	1.0	1.6209
RESTRICT	.7940	3.0	2.3820	-1.1177	3.0	-3.3531	-.3339	3.0	-1.0017
CUTASIAN	-4.6004	1.0	-4.6004	-1.1228	1.0	-1.1228	-1.1431	1.0	-1.1431
MIXED	-.6957	3.0	-2.0871	-1.3160	3.0	-3.9480	1.1418	3.0	3.4254
ANTIYUGO	-1.1114	1.0	-1.1114	1.1132	1.0	1.1132	.3781	1.0	.3781
ANTINEUT	1.4387	1.0	1.4387	1.4387	1.0	1.0422	.2000	1.0	.2000
discriminant score			2.2539			-3.2225			-.8977

center around the locations of the group centroids, the "most typical" positions for each group. These can be computed by using the group means in the formulas. For Bardes's data, the four group centroids have the following location, in order by group number: (1.74, –.94, .02), (–6.93, –.60, .28), (–1.48, .69, –.30), and (1.86, 2.06, .25). Although we can tell that none of the centroids is close to another, we could better visualize their locations if we were to plot them.

Two-Function Plots

When there are two discriminant functions, we can easily plot the location of the centroids and data cases. In our example, we have three functions but a two-function plot will still be very informative, especially when we consider that the first two functions are most important. Figure 2 is such a plot. The asterisks denote the four group centroids, while the numbers symbolize Senators from the group with that number. Senator Aiken is in group 1 (pro-aid) and is represented by the "1" closest to the lower-right corner. Senator Bridges is the highest "4" on the plot (near the asterisk).

An examination of this plot tells us that the groups are quite distinct. The centroids are well-separated and there is no obvious overlap of the individual cases, even though a couple Senators from group 1 are straying close to group 4. (In the next chapter we will take a closer look at these individuals.) Groups 1 and 4 hold nearly the same positions on the first function. Both have a preference for spending more on foreign aid. They are very different, however, on the second function, being at opposite ends of the continuum concerning more (positive aid) or fewer (negative aid) restrictions on the foreign aid programs. The lines drawn on this plot delineate classification "territories" which will be discussed in the next chapter.

Plots such as Figure 2 can be very helpful when there is very little overlap among the groups. As the groups become less distinct, especially if the number of cases is large, plotting all the cases produces a blur. In that situation, it may be more informative to examine a plot of only the centroids or separate plots for each group.

As the number of discriminant functions increases, we will have progressively more difficulty visualizing the locations of the centroids. Of course, one could prepare a physical model for three functions, but four or more cannot be represented. Because the first two functions are the most powerful discriminators, a plot based on just these two functions can be very informative if not sufficient in itself.

28

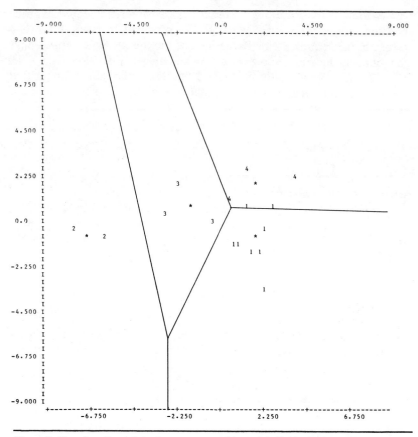

Figure 2: **Two-function plot of group centroids and individual cases. The horizontal dimension represents function 1 while the vertical dimension represents function 2.**

One-Function Plots

When there is only one discriminant function, we can arrange the data cases along a straight line. This would tell us what portions of the function are "occupied," but it would not give us a very good notion of the density of points, especially when there are a large number of cases.

An alternative strategy is to prepare a histogram for each group. First we divide the continuum into small intervals of .1 standard deviation, for example, or whatever seems appropriate. Then an "X," or some other symbol for the case, such as the group number, is placed at each interval containing a data case. For the second and subsequent cases falling into an interval, the "X's" are stacked one atop the other so that the height of the stack denotes the number of cases in that interval. A quick glance can then tell us the density and distribution of the group. By placing the group histograms above one another, we can compare the relative locations of the groups.

If we were to examine Bardes's data only on the first function, we would get the plot shown in Figure 3. With such a small number of cases, this plot is not very interesting and does not really illustrate a histogram because there are so few cases in the same intervals. We can see, however, that on this single dimension there is not much difference between the areas occupied by groups 1 and 4. In fact, their centroids occupy the same position. A much better example of a one-dimensional plot can be seen in Heyck and Klecka (1973: 172) which has been reproduced in the SPSS manual (Nie et al., 1975: 439).

Standardized Coefficients

When we shift the focus of our attention from individual cases and group centroids to discovering the contributions of the individual variables, we must go beyond the unstandardized coefficients. While the unstandardized coefficients do tell us the *absolute* contribution of a variable in determining the discriminant score, this information may be misleading when the meaning of one unit change in the value of a variable is not the same from one variable to another (i.e., when the standard deviations are not the same). If we want to know the *relative* importance of the variable, we need to look at standardized coefficients.

Standardized coefficients are the ones that would be obtained in Equation 5 if the original data all had standard deviations of 1.0, which could be achieved by converting the raw data into standard form.[10] Rather than converting the raw data and recomputing the coefficients, we can compute the standardized coefficients (c's) from the unstandardized coefficients (u's) by using the following transformation:

$$c_i = u_i \sqrt{\frac{w_{ii}}{n. - g}} \qquad [7]$$

where w_{ii} is the sum of squares for variable i (as defined in Equation 3), n. is the total number of cases, and g is the number of groups. The standardized coefficients are helpful, because we can use them to determine which variables contribute most to determining scores on the function. This is done by examining the magnitude of the standardized coefficients

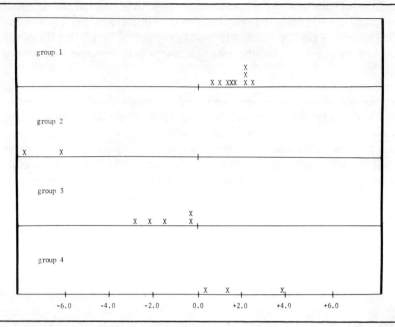

Figure 3: Group histograms for Bardes data. Each "X" denotes one Senator. The horizontal axis is the first canonical discriminant function measured in standard deviation units.

(ignoring the sign): The larger the magnitude, the greater is that variable's contribution.

Table 6 reports the standardized coefficients for the Senate roll call data. For Function 1, we see that CUTASIAN makes the greatest contribution. All of the other variables are of minor importance compared to CUTASIAN. ANTINEUT and ANTIYUGO are the next in rank order. About all that can be said for them is that they contribute approximately twice as much as MIXED.

On Function 2, four of the six variables (RESTRICT, MIXED, ANTIYUGO, and ANTINEUT) have relatively high standardized coefficients. So each makes a somewhat similar contribution to the discriminant function on this dimension. CUTAID followed by MIXED are the dominant variables on the third function.[11]

If we wanted to do so, we could compute discriminant scores from the standardized coefficients. However, we would have to multiply them by data values in standard form (z scores).[12]

TABLE 6
Standardized Discriminant Coefficients

Variable	Standardized Coefficient		
	Function 1	Function 2	Function 3
CUTAID	.6094	−.3942	1.2227
RESTRICT	.7068	−.9950	−.2973
CUTASIAN	−2.1859	−.5335	−.5432
MIXED	−.4760	−.9004	.7812
ANTIYUGO	−.8077	.8090	.2748
ANTINEUT	1.0168	.7365	.1414

Structure Coefficients

To determine the similarity between a single variable and a discriminant function, we can look at the product-moment correlation between the two. These correlations are called "total structure coefficients." As correlations, they can be considered to be the cosines for the angles formed by the variables and the function. Thus, by knowing these coefficients, we know the geometric structure of the data space.[13]

A structure coefficient tells us how closely a variable and a function are related. When the absolute magnitude of the coefficient is very large (near +1.0 or −1.0), the function is carrying nearly the same information as the variable. When the coefficient is near zero, they have very little in common. We can "name" a function on the basis of the structure coefficients by noting the variables having the highest coefficients. If those variables seem to be measuring a similar characteristic, we could name the function after that characteristic.

As an example, consider the structure coefficients reported in Table 7 for the Senate roll call data. On Function 1, CUTAID and CUTASIAN are the dominant variables. Their negative signs suggest that we might refer to Function 1 as the "pro-aid" dimension. For Function 2 we see that the last three variables all have high structure coefficients. These deal with prohibitions on aid to countries not allied with the United States, so we could call this the "anti-aid to non-allies" dimension. Function 3 does not have any large coefficients, which makes it difficult to interpret. RESTRICT and CUTAID have the largest coefficients here but they have opposite signs. By looking at the location of the group centroids on this function, we may get some helpful information. Groups 2 and 4 (oppose aid and anticommunists) are at the positive end; group 3 (opposed to

TABLE 7
Total Structure Coefficients

Variable	Structure Coefficient		
	Function 1	Function 2	Function 3
CUTAID	−.565	.355	.326
RESTRICT	.345	.260	−.429
CUTASIAN	−.858	.241	−.160
MIXED	.269	−.671	.254
ANTIYUGO	−.293	.785	.076
ANTINEUT	−.140	.751	−.269

foreign involvements) is at the negative end; and group 1 (pro-aid) is in the middle. This implies that Function 3 serves to differentiate between different types of opposition to foreign aid.

The structure coefficients we have been discussing here are based on total correlations and are best referred to as "total structure coefficients." They are useful for identifying the kind of information carried by the functions which is useful for discriminating *between* groups. Sometimes, however, we are interested in knowing how the functions are related to the variables *within* the groups. This information can be obtained from the pooled within-groups correlations—called "within-groups structure coefficients"—which can be calculated as follows:

$$s'_{ij} = \sum_{k=1}^{p} r'_{ik} c_{kj} = \sum_{k=1}^{p} \frac{w_{ik} c_{kj}}{\sqrt{w_{ii} w_{kk}}} \qquad [8]$$

where s'_{ij} = within-groups structure coefficient for variable i and function j;

r'_{ik} = pooled within-groups correlation coefficient between variables i and k;

c_{kj} = standardized canonical discriminant function coefficient for variable k on function j.

Table 8 gives the within structure coefficients for the roll call data. Notice that these coefficients are smaller than the total structure coefficients but the rankings from the largest absolute magnitude to the smallest are similar (although not identical). This is a typical result but not a necessary condition. Some of the within coefficients could be larger or much smaller or even have the opposite sign from their total counterparts. And

TABLE 8
Within Structure Coefficients

Variable	Within Structure Coefficient		
	Function 1	Function 2	Function 3
CUTAID	−.218	.279	.392
RESTRICT	.115	.176	−.461
CUTASIAN	−.483	.276	−.299
MIXED	.102	−.516	.315
ANTIYUGO	−.121	.662	.087
ANTINEUT	−.054	.588	−.340

the rankings could be very different. These two sets of coefficients report on different kinds of structures, so we should not expect them to yield the same interpretation, except when all the group centroids are identical.

Structure coefficients tell us something quite different from what is communicated by the standardized coefficients. The standardized coefficients give us the variable's contribution to calculating the discriminant *score*. This is one way of looking at the variable's importance, but it has a serious limitation. If two variables share nearly the same discriminating information (i.e., if they are highly correlated), they must share their contribution to the score even if that joint contribution is very important. Consequently, their standardized coefficients may be smaller than when only one of the variables is used. Or, the standardized coefficients might be larger but with opposite signs, so that the contribution of one is partially cancelled by the opposite contribution of the other.[14] This is because the standardized coefficients take into consideration the simultaneous contributions of all the other variables.

The structure coefficients, however, are simple bivariate correlations, so they are not affected by relationships with the other variables. Notice that CUTAID had a low standardized coefficient on Function 1 but a relatively large total structure coefficient. This is probably due to the very high correlation between CUTAID and CUTASIAN (.787). What is happening is that CUTASIAN is making a large negative contribution to the discriminant score while CUTAID is making a small positive contribution so that the net effect represents their true effect upon the score. The structure coefficients also help us understand the contribution of ANTIYUGO and ANTINEUT to Function 1. These two variables have rather small structure coefficients which means they have very little in common with the function. This is a different impression than we got from the standardized coefficients which were rather large and with opposite signs. These two variables are highly correlated (.767), so we see they are both making large contributions in opposite directions which cancel out each other. The perverse tendency of such situations to arise in discriminant analysis implies that the structure coefficients are a better guide to the meaning of the canonical discriminant functions than the standardized coefficients are.

Overall and Klett (1972: 292-295) show how structure coefficients can be used to graphically observe the differences between group centroids when there are two canonical discriminant functions. On a graph with axes defined by the two functions, they plot the group centroids and the grand centroid. From the grand centroid they draw an arrow for each discriminating variable at an angle calculated from the structure coefficients. The length of the arrow is determined by the between-groups and within-group variances for that variable. The resulting diagram gives a visual impression of how the groups differ on the discriminating variables and the potency of those variables.

How Many Functions Are Significant?

In Chapter 2, I showed that the solution to Equation 4 yielded an eigenvalue (the lambda) and a set of coefficients for each canonical discriminant function. The number of possible solutions to the general problem is actually equal to the number of discriminating variables, p. Some of these, however, will be mathematically trivial solutions, and others may lack statistical significance. All of the lambdas will be positive or zero, and the larger that lambda is, the more the groups will be separated on that function. Thus, the function with the largest eigenvalue is the most powerful discriminator, while the function with the smallest eigenvalue is the weakest.

THE NUMBER OF FUNCTIONS

An uninteresting solution to Equation 4 is to let lambda equal zero. Such a solution would be useless, because it implies no differences between the groups on that function. However, when p is less than $(g - 1)$, we do get $(p - g + 1)$ solutions that have an eigenvalue of zero. This is why the maximum number of canonical discriminant functions, q, is the smaller of the two numbers p and $(g - 1)$. Referring back to the Senate roll call example, $p = 6$, $(g - 1) = 3$, so $q = 3$. Out of the q possible solutions we may still get eigenvalues that are exactly zero. This happens in those degenerate cases in which one or more of the centroids fits into the space defined by the others. More typically, the fit will not be exact due to sampling or measurement error. Rather, the eigenvalue will be a small number. The question is: How small does lambda have to be before we consider it to be the result of sampling or measurement error rather than a truly different dimension? This is the question of statistical significance. Even when a function is statistically significant, we may decide that it lacks substantive importance, because it does not discriminate among the groups well enough.

Before learning how to test for significance, let us take a look at the eigenvalues from the Senate roll call example. Table 9 gives these results. As expected, there are three nonzero eigenvalues, and they have been presented in the order of descending magnitude. This is customary, because the size of the eigenvalue is related to the discriminating power of that function: The larger the eigenvalue, the greater the discrimination. By placing them in descending order, we know that the first function is the most powerful; the second function provides the greatest discrimination *after* the first has done its best; the third provides the greatest further discrimination *after* the first and second have done their best; and so on. Taken together, all the functions do not necessarily provide perfect discrimination, but at least we know the order of importance.

THE RELATIVE PERCENTAGE

The actual numbers representing the eigenvalues are not of any immediately obvious value to us. They cannot be interpreted directly. When there is more than one function, though, we do want to compare the relative magnitudes to see how much of the total discriminating power each has. Thus, 9.65976 for the first eigenvalue is more than six times larger than the eigenvalue for the second function. And the fact that the first eigenvalue is 180 times bigger than the third tells us that the third function is very weak indeed.

TABLE 9
Eigenvalues and Measures of Importance

Canonical Discriminant Function	Eigenvalue	Relative Percentage	Canonical Correlation
1	9.65976	85.54	.952
2	1.57922	13.98	.782
3	.05357	.47	.225

To help make such comparisons, we can convert the eigenvalues into relative percentages. This is done by first summing all the eigenvalues to get a measure of the total discriminating power. We then divide this result into each individual eigenvalue. Thus, the first function contains 85.54% of the total discriminating power in this system of equations.

The third function in this example illustrates the situation in which a function is so unimportant that it appears to lack research utility. When a function carries such a miniscule proportion of the total discriminating power, it is unlikely to contribute to our understanding of group differences beyond what we learn from the other functions. There is no rule stating how large the relative percentage must be before the function is of interest to us, so Function 2 may also prove deficient when examined further. Even Function 1 could lack substantive significance[15] (according to criteria to be discussed later), even though it is the most powerful of the three. All that the relative percentages can tell us is whether that function is so weak *relative to the others* that it is unlikely to add further to our understanding of the differences between the groups.

THE CANONICAL CORRELATION

Another way to judge the substantive utility of a discriminant function is by examining the canonical correlation coefficient. This coefficient is a measure of association which summarizes the degree of relatedness between the groups and the discriminant function. A value of zero denotes no relationship at all, while large numbers (always positive) represent increasing degrees of association with 1.0 being the maximum. The canonical correlation, which we can symbolize by r*, is related to the eigenvalue by the following formula:

$$r_i^* = \sqrt{\frac{\lambda_i}{1 + \lambda_i}} \qquad [9]$$

where i denotes the relevant discriminant function.

The canonical correlation coefficient comes from the statistical technique called canonical correlation analysis (see Levine, 1977). Canonical correlation is a way to study the relationships between two separate sets of interval level variables. The analysis is done by creating q pairs of linear combinations, where q is the number of variables in the smaller set. The linear combinations in a given pair, one from each set, are derived to maximize the correlation between them. The first pair has the greatest degree of association; the second pair has the next greatest degree of association under the condition that they be uncorrelated with the first; and so on. The canonical correlation coefficient is, of course, the measure of association, and it is identical to the Pearson product-moment correlation between the two linear combinations in the pair.

With a little mathematical sleight of hand we can convert discriminant analysis (at least the part we are discussing here) into canonical correlation analysis. Obviously, the discriminating variables comprise one of the "sets." Then, if we represent the groups by (g – 1) dichotomies (known as "dummy variables"), we have the other "set." From this we get q pairs of linear combinations, where the discriminant function represents half the pair and the combination representing the groups is never actually derived. The canonical correlation coefficients then have the interpretation presented above as the measure of association between the two sets acting through the pairs of linear combinations. It is this analogy which leads some statisticians to refer to the canonical discriminant function as a "canonical variate."[16]

An alternative interpretation of the canonical correlation coefficient comes from analysis of variance (Iversen and Norpoth, 1976: 30-32), where it goes under the names of "eta" and the "correlation ratio." Here, the groups are considered as an independent variable which influences the values on the discriminant function, the dependent variable. The degree of difference between the group means on the function is measured by eta. A more intuitive interpretation of eta can be made when it is squared. Eta-squared (i.e., the canonical correlation squared) is the proportion of variation in the discriminant function explained by the groups.

Regardless of which approach is taken, the canonical correlation can be a valuable tool in judging the substantive utility of the discriminant function. A high coefficient, such as found for the first function in Table 9, indicates that a strong relationship exists between the groups and the first discriminant function. The third function, however, has a rather low value, which indicates a weak association, as surmised from the relative percentage.[17]

On the basis of Table 9, one should not jump to the conclusion that the first discriminant function will always have a large canonical correlation. Even though the first function is always the "most" powerful in a relative sense (as measured by the relative percentage), it may only be weakly related to the groups (as measured by the canonical correlations). For this reason, the canonical correlation is more useful to us, because it reports how well the discriminant function is doing. If the groups are not very different on the variables being analyzed, then all of the correlations will be low, because we cannot create discrimination when none already existed. By examining both the relative percentage and the canonical correlation, we can determine fairly well how many discriminant functions are substantively meaningful and how much utility they have in explaining group differences.

MEASURING RESIDUAL DISCRIMINATION WITH WILKS'S LAMBDA

So far, we have discussed the number of discriminant functions in terms of mathematical limits and substantive importance. These considerations apply without regard to the sampling properties of the data. They are equally appropriate with population data[18] as well as any type of sample. If we are analyzing population data, then the questions of the number of functions and their importance have been settled by the relative percentage and the canonical correlation. Within the limits of measurement error, these statistics completely describe the degree of discrimination between the groups and the discriminating variables.

When the data are from a sample, as opposed to constituting the entire population, an additional question must be raised. What is the probability that the sampling process produced cases which show the computed degree of discrimination when in fact there are no group differences in the population? This is the question of statistical significance, and it is appropriate only when dealing with samples.[19] Actually, we can answer questions of statistical significance only when the sampling process has a probability basis. For many statistics, the tests of significance apply only to simple random samples due to the complexity of deriving tests for other sampling situations. Thus, the discussion here will assume simple random sampling. In the event the cases were drawn by some other sampling procedure, the best advice is to interpret the tests conservatively and place greater emphasis upon the substantive importance of the results.

The most common test for the statistical significance of the discriminant functions proceeds indirectly. Rather than testing the function itself, we examine the residual discrimination in the system *prior* to deriving that function. By "residual discrimination," we mean the ability of the variables to discriminate among the groups beyond the information that has been extracted by the previously computed functions. If the residual discrimination is too small, then it is meaningless to derive any more functions, even if they exist mathematically. To understand this notion better, let us take a look at the statistic used to measure discrimination, Wilks's lambda (also called the U statistic).

Wilks's lambda is a multivariate measure of group differences over several variables (the discriminating variables). Although there are several ways to calculate this measure, the formula which is most appropriate in the present context is:

$$\Lambda = \prod_{i=k+1}^{q} \frac{1}{1 + \lambda_i} \qquad [10]$$

where k denotes the number of functions already derived, and the symbol Π means that the individual terms are to be multiplied to yield the final product.

To illustrate the application of the symbol Π, we can compute the value of Wilks's lambda for the Senate roll call data before any functions have been derived. In this instance, k = 0. From Table 9 we get:

$$\Lambda = \left(\frac{1}{1 + 9.65976} \right) \left(\frac{1}{1 + 1.57922} \right) \left(\frac{1}{1 + .05357} \right)$$

$$= (.09381)(.38771)(.94915) = .03452.$$

Because lambda is an "inverse" measure, this outcome means that the six scales used are extremely effective in differentiating among the groups. Values of lambda which are near zero denote high discrimination (i.e., the group centroids are greatly separated and very distinct relative to the amount of dispersion within the groups). As lambda increases toward its maximum value of 1.0, it is reporting progressively *less* discrimination. When lambda equals 1.0, the group centroids are identical (no group differences).

Obviously, the four groups of Senators are very different on the selected scales, so it is reasonable to begin deriving discriminant functions. After the first (and most powerful) function has been derived, it has removed a good deal of the discriminating information from the system. We now want to inquire whether enough residual discrimination remains to justify the derivation of the second function. From Table 10 we see Wilks's lambda now equals .3680 (for k = 1), which is still small. Removing the second function depletes the discriminating information further, so that lambda becomes .9492 for k = 2. This value is very high, indicating that the remaining information about group differences may not be worth pursuing. We saw similar indications when we examined the relative percentages and the canonical correlations. So most analysts would conclude that the remaining discriminant functions (in this case, only one) are either unimportant or statistically spurious.

TABLE 10
Residual Discrimination and Test of Significance

Functions Derived, k	Wilks's Lambda	Chi-Square	Degrees of Freedom	Significance Level
0	.0345	43.760	18	.001
1	.3680	12.996	10	.224
2	.9492	.678	4	.954

TESTING THE SIGNIFICANCE OF WILKS'S LAMBDA

Our discussion of Wilks's lambda so far has presented it as another measure of association. One can use it for that purpose, but its inverse denotation and its emphasis on the residual discrimination make it less useful than the relative percentage and canonical correlation. Lambda, however, can be converted into a test of significance. Thus, we employ it as an intermediate statistic, rather than the desired end product.

We test the significance of lambda by converting it into an approximation of either the chi-square or F distributions.[20] These can be compared to standard tables to determine the significance level, and some computer programs print the exact signficance level. Chi-square is easier to calculate in this situation and is based on the following formula:

$$\chi^2 = - \left[n. - \left(\frac{p+g}{2} \right) - 1 \right] \log_e \Lambda_k \qquad [11]$$

with $(p-k)(g-k-1)$ degrees of freedom.

Table 10 gives the chi-square results for the example data.[21] As anticipated, the group differences are definitely signficant *before* the derivation of any discriminant functions (k = 0). The significance level of .001 tells us that we would get a chi-square this large or larger only one time out of a thousand samples when there actually were no differences between the centroids (assuming independent, simple random samples). Given this unlikely event, we are safe in assuming that the results did come from a population which did have differences between the groups. This also tells us that at least our first function will be statistically significant.

After deriving the first function, we check again to see if the remaining discrimination is significant. Naturally, the chi-square is smaller, and the significance level is .224 (k = 1). Most researchers would consider this result *not* significant, so we would not derive the second and third functions on the presumption that all of the significant information about group differences had already been absorbed. The implication is that a single dimension can represent all of the observed differences between the groups. A second dimension (which would create a plane) would not add any differences which we could confidently say exist in the population.

If we had found instead that the residual discrimination was significant, we would proceed to derive the second function. Then we would repeat the process of checking the new residual discrimination (for k = 2). In this instance, the significance level is so large (.954) that no one would deem the remaining discrimination to be significant. Thus, there is abolutely no sense in deriving the third function, because it could not possibly add to explaining the group differences. This finding helps explain why we had so much difficulty interpreting the structure coefficients for Function 3 and why there were not very large differences among the group centroids on that function.

Although this example has fewer statistically significant functions than are mathematically allowed, this is not always the case. In many situations, the last look at the residual discrimination (for k = g – 1) shows that a significant amount remains; therefore, we would want to derive all the possible functions, unless there are other reasons for not doing so (such as a low canonical correlation). The rationale is that we continue deriving functions until the residual discrimination becomes nonsignificant. This assures us that the derived functions are statistically significant *as a set*. It does not tell us the significance of any single function (unless only one has been derived), but rather it gives the significance of all derived functions working together. This is quite satisfactory, because we use them as a set and our objective is to reduce the discriminating information to the smallest number of dimensions. The only real problem comes when we find that the total set of discriminating information is nonsignificant (i.e., when k = 0). This can quickly destroy a research project unless the original objective was to show that the groups were not different after all.

For pedagogical reasons, this chapter has proceeded in reverse order from what an analyst would normally do. Logically, a researcher should ask first, "Which, if any, of my functions are statistically and substantively significant?" One need not pursue further analysis of any functions which are eliminated. For the remaining functions, the researcher should combine an examination of the structure coefficients with the group centroid positions to discover the meaning of each function. The structure coefficients also reveal information about how each variable contributes to discrimination along that dimension.

In some research situations the analyst's job will be finished once the canonical discriminant functions have been interpreted. More likely, the researcher will proceed to classify cases—either for practical or analytical purposes—which is the topic of the next chapter.

4. CLASSIFICATION PROCEDURES

At the beginning of this paper, I divided the purpose of discriminant analysis into two activities: interpretation and classification. So far I have focused primary attention on interpretation, which concerns the number and importance of the canonical discriminant functions to be derived and the interpretation of their meaning for explaining group differences. Classification is a separate activity in which either the discriminating variables or the canonical discriminant functions are used to predict the group to which a case most likely belongs. Several classification procedures exist, but they all use the notion of comparing the case's position to each of the group centroids in order to locate the "closest" one. For example, Bardes's intention in her research was to use the 19 Senators with identifiable factional positions to create the canonical discriminant function subspace. She then calculated discriminant scores for the remaining Senators so that she could assign them to one of the four groups on the basis of their roll call votes. In this way she could study the size and composition of the factions and the ways in which they changed over time.

Classification Functions

Classification is the process by which a decision is made that a specific case "belongs to" or "most closely resembles" one particular group. This decision is based on the information carried by the discriminating variables. There are several ways in which classification can be performed. They typically involve defining some notion of "distance" between the case and each group centroid with the case being classified into the "closest" group.

These classification procedures can use either the discriminating variables by themselves or the canonical discriminant functions. In the first instance, one is not performing a "discriminant analysis" at all.[22] This activity merely uses the theory of maximum group differences to derive classification functions. No tests are made for the significance of the discrimination or the dimensionality of the discriminant space. When the canonical discriminant functions are derived first and classification is based upon them, we can perform a more thorough analysis. We will elaborate on this last point later, but for now we will pursue the topic of classification on the assumption the discriminating variables are used directly.

SIMPLE CLASSIFICATION FUNCTIONS

Fisher (1936) was the first to suggest that classification should be based on a linear combination of the discriminating variables. He proposed using a linear combination which maximizes group differences while minimizing variation within the groups. An adaptation of his proposal leads us to derive a separate linear combination, called a "classification function," for each group. These have the following form:

$$h_k = b_{k0} + b_{k1}X_1 + b_{k2}X_2 + \ldots + b_{kp}X_p \qquad [12]$$

where h_k is the score for group k and the b's are coefficients that need to be derived. A case is classified into the group with the highest score (largest h). The coefficients for these classification functions are derived by the following computation:

$$b_{ki} = (n.-g) \sum_{j=1}^{p} a_{ij}X_{jk.} \qquad [13]$$

where b_{ki} is the coefficient for variable i in the equation corresponding to group k, and a_{ij} is an element from the inverse of the within-groups sum of crossproducts matrix (W).[23] A constant term is also required and defined as:

$$b_{k0} = -.5 \sum_{j=1}^{p} b_{kj}X_{jk.} \qquad [14]$$

We do not usually interpret these classification function coefficients, because they are not standardized and there is a different function for each group. The scores also lack intrinsic value because they are arbitrary numbers which have the property that the case resembles most closely that group on which it has the highest score. I will refer to the functions described by Equation 12 as "simple classification functions," because they only assume equal group covariance matrices and do not employ any of the adjustments to be discussed later in this chapter.

As an illustration of how these functions are employed, consider Table 11 which gives the coefficients for the Senate roll call data. By applying these coefficients to Senator Aiken's raw data values, we get scores of 89.742, 46.578, 78.101, and 78.221 for the four groups. Because the first score is the largest, we would classify Aiken into the first group (which is, in fact, a correct prediction).

GENERALIZED DISTANCE FUNCTIONS

A more intuitive means of classification is to measure the distances from the individual case to each of the group centroids and classify the case into the closest group. However, when the variables are correlated and do not have the same measurement units and standard deviations, the concept of "distance" is not well-defined. Mahalanobis (1963), an Indian statistician, has proposed a generalized distance measure which solves this problem. We can use it in the following form:

$$D^2(X|G_k) = (n.-g) \sum_{i=1}^{p} \sum_{j=1}^{p} a_{ij}(X_i - X_{ik.})(X_j - X_{jk.}) \qquad [15]$$

where $D^2(X|G_k)$ is the squared distance from point X (a specific case) to the centroid of group k. After calculating D^2 for each group, we would classify the case into the group with the smallest D^2. That group is the one in which the typical profile on the discriminating variables most closely resembles the profile of this case. If the distance to the closest group is large, the profiles may match rather poorly, but they are a better match than for any other group.

TABLE 11
Simple Classification Coefficients

Variable	Group 1	Group 2	Group 3	Group 4
CUTAID	13.040	6.283	9.064	11.941
RESTRICT	5.755	−1.600	1.485	2.424
CUTASIAN	20.056	59.286	33.452	15.886
MIXED	37.016	42.909	36.761	33.253
ANTIYUGO	−2.639	7.480	2.634	.652
ANTINEUT	8.559	−3.516	5.542	11.897
Constant	−77.587	−146.882	−87.329	−69.186

Equation 15 assumes that the groups have equal covariance matrices. If this assumption is not satisfied, the equation can be modified as described by Tatsuoka (1971: 222).

PROBABILITY OF GROUP MEMBERSHIP

As it turns out, D^2 has the same properties as the chi-square statistic with p degrees of freedom. Thus, we are measuring the distance in "chi-square units." If we can assume that each group comes from a population with a multivariate normal distribution, we know that most of the cases will be clustered near the centroid and that the density of cases will diminish in a precise fashion as we get further away from the centroid. By knowing the distance from the centroid, we can tell the proportion of the group's population that is closer and the proportion that is further away. The latter proportion is the probability that a case located that far away actually belongs to the group. Because our distances are measured in chi-square units, we can test them for significance to obtain this probability. Let us denote this probability as $Pr(X|G_k)$, which is the probability that a case that far from the centroid would actually belong to group k.

By classifying a case into the closest group according to D^2, we are implicitly assigning it to the group for which it has the highest probability of belonging. By looking at the probabilities, we can say more about the case than that it is "closest" to some particular group. The case may actually have a high probability of "belonging to" more than one group or to none of the groups. Consider the situation in which discrimination is low and the groups overlap a great deal. Here, a case at the centroid of group 1 might still have a very high probability of "belonging to" group 2, because it is also "close" to group 2. Indeed, this is an additional test of the discriminating power of the discriminant variables being used. Another important situation is when the case is very far from all the groups—that is, when all of the probabilities are small. For us to classify this case into the nearest group might be meaningless, because it has so little resemblance to the other cases in that group. Senator Aiken is an example of this situation. His probability of belonging to group 1 (the closest group) is only .10, which is very small. On the other hand, Senator Bridges has a relatively high .48 probability of belonging to his closest group (group 4).

Clearly, these distance probabilities for all the groups need not sum to 1.0 for any given case. If we assume, however, that every case must belong to one of the groups, we can compute a probability of group membership for each group. The probability that case X is a member of a group k is:

$$Pr(G_k \mid X) = \frac{Pr(X \mid G_k)}{\sum_{i=1}^{g} Pr(X \mid G_i)} \qquad [16]$$

These probabilities, often called *posterior* probabilities, do sum to 1.0 over all the groups, and classification on the largest of these values also is equivalent to using the smallest distance. For our Senators, Aiken has a posterior probability of 1.00 (after rounding) of belonging to group 1, and Bridges has a posterior probability of .99 for group 4.

Note the differences in the interpretation of these two probabilities. The posterior values, $Pr(G_k \mid X)$, give the probability that the case belongs to group k. But $Pr(X \mid G_k)$ is an estimate of the proportion of cases in that group's population which are further from the centroid than X is.

Adjusting for Prior Probabilities
or Cost of Misclassification

So far, the discussion of classification has assumed that each group is to be treated equally. This may not always be desirable in practice. Consider, for example, a two-group situation in which 90% of the total population belongs to group 1. Before doing any calculations, we know that there is a very high probability that any given case belongs to group 1. Therefore, one would want to classify it into group 2 only if the evidence was very strong that it belongs there. This can be done by adjusting the posterior probabilities to account for prior knowledge of probable group membership.

Another situation in which we might want to adjust the posterior probabilites is when the "cost" of misclassification differs dramatically from one group to the next. By cost, I mean the practical implication of assigning a case to a particular group, as measured in terms of money, suffering, or other consequences. A typical example would be the use of classification functions to determine whether a cancer is malignant or benign based on various symptoms. While the patient is likely to endure greater suffering whenever an error in classification is made, the patient with malignant cancer that is diagnosed as benign will suffer more than the patient with benign cancer that is diagnosed as malignant. If these costs of misclassification can be expressed in relative terms as proportions, they can be used in a fashion similar to prior probabilities.

Both of these examples are situations in which we might want to incorporate prior probabilities into the classification function in order to improve the accuracy of prediction or minimize the net cost of making errors. This adjustment is made to the simple classification functions by adding the natural logarithm of the prior probability for that group to the group's constant term. Or we can modify the chi-square distance (D^2) by subtracting two times the natural logarithm of the prior probability. The change in the chi-square distance is mathematically identical to multiplying $Pr(X|G_k)$ by the prior probability for that group. Tatsuoka (1971: 217-232) and Cooley and Lohnes (1971: 262-270) give a more complete discussion of these modifications.

If the groups are very distinct, adjustments for prior probabilities are unlikely to affect classification results, because very few cases will be near the borderlines between the groups. Thus, prior probabilities will have their greatest impact when the groups overlap such that many cases may otherwise have a high probability of belonging to more than one group. Of course, the decision to employ prior probabilities should be made on theoretical grounds. If there is no theoretical reason to use them, we are usually better off not doing so. Also keep in mind that prior probabilities based on *population* sizes need not be the same as the *sample* proportions.

Classification Based on Canonical Discriminant Functions

Classification can also be done with the canonical discriminant functions instead of using the original discriminating variables. The same formulas apply except that the X's are replaced by f's. And the final classifications will generally be identical.

When a large number of cases need to be classified by the distance or probability methods, we reduce our work considerably by using the discriminant functions. Instead of computing the distances for p variables, we need to use only the q canonical discriminant functions; this usually means fewer mathematical operations, even though the discriminant functions have to be derived. If the simple classification functions are being employed, however, using the canonical discriminant functions would entail more labor.

There are certain conditions under which the classifications will not necessarily be the same when using the canonical discriminant functions. One of these is when the group covariance matrices are not equal. This is because the procedure for deriving the canonical discriminant functions must use the within-groups crossproducts matrix which is a weighted average of the individual group crossproduct matrices. Thus, the transformation is not exact. Unfortunately, there is no clear guideline for determining how different the group matrices must be before the use of discriminant functions becomes unjustified. Tatsuoka (1971: 232-233) reports evidence that the canonical discriminant function procedure yields closely similar results and can be used unless the group covariance matrices are "drastically" different.

Another situation in which the two procedures may yield different results is when one or more of the canonical discriminant functions are ignored because they are not statistically significant. While some cases may be classified differently in this instance, the canonical discriminant function results should be more accurate, because the effect of idiosyncratic sample variation has been reduced.

Bardes employed only two of the three discriminant functions for the classification in her study and did not make any adjustment for prior probabilities. Her data show that Pr(Aiken|group 1) = .064. This is a very small probability reflecting Aiken's position on the extreme edge of group 1. The probabilities for each of the other groups, however, are essentially zero, so we would classify Aiken into group 1 which agrees with the results from the simple classification functions. By looking back at Figure 2, we can also see that Senator Aiken is obviously closest to the group 1 centroid (he is the "1" furthest to the lower right).

Now let us take a closer look at the two cases from group 1 which are located about midway between the group 1 and group 4 centroids. These are Senators Capehart (R, Ind.) on the right and Knowland (R, Calif.) on the left. Here, Pr(group 1|Capehart) = .262, but Pr(group 4|Capehart) = .738. This implies that Capehart's voting behavior is more similar to that of group 4, even though Bardes had originally assigned him to group 1 on the basis of other substantive evidence. For Knowland, the probability of membership in group 1 is .538 and in group 4 is .436. These probabilities are so similar that one might hesitate about making a classification choice. When a case is on the borderline, we may want to leave it as ambiguous and unclassifiable. Indeed, Bardes reviewed the substantive evidence on Knowland and concluded that it was not sufficiently strong to keep him as a definite member of either group, so she withdrew him from the analysis. She also reexamined Capehart's record and decided that group 4 was more appropriate for him, so she changed his group code. After making these adjustments, she performed the analysis anew and proceeded to classify all of the Senators on the basis of the new discriminant functions.

Territorial Plots

To get a better picture of how cases are being classified, we can super-impose the classification boundary lines over our plot of cases. Back in Figure 2, the straight lines separating the groups represent these bound-aries. The nearly horizonal line at the right divides groups 4 and 1. A case located above the line is closer to the group 4 centroid, while cases below the line are closer to the group 1 centroid. In a similar fashion, the other lines demarcate the territories wherein a case would be classified into the enclosed group. Of course, when the discrimination is weak, many cases may fall outside of the territory for their group. These cases will be mis-classified according to the decision rules enunciated earlier.

We can also divide up one-dimensional plots and histograms. When we have more than two dimensions, however, territorial plots are not practical because of the impossibility of representing such a space on a sheet of paper. This is another advantage of classifying with discriminant func-tions—most research situations involve only one or two functions (which can be plotted easily) even though they are based on many discriminating variables.

For the one-function case, the dividing point between two groups is one half the sum of the discriminant scores for the two group centroids. When there are two functions, our calculations become more difficult but the algebra is straightforward. Essentially, we have to use Equation 16 to solve for the situation in which $D^2(X|G_i) = D^2(X|G_j)$. The solution is an equation for a straight line. These rules presume that we are treating the individual group covariance matrices as identical. If this is not the case, we have to make appropriate accommodations. In the one-function situ-ation, the dividing point will be closer to the group with the smaller vari-ance. When we have two functions, the boundary will be a curve which tends to wrap around the group with the smaller dispersion (see Van de Geer, 1971: 263-265).

The Classification Matrix

Although researchers generally engage in classification as a means of predicting the group membership for cases of "unknown" membership, we can also use it to test the accuracy of the classsification procedure. We do this by taking "known" cases (those used to derive the classification functions) and applying the classification rule to them. The proportion of cases correctly classified indicates the accuracy of the procedure and indirectly confirms the degree of group separation. We can prepare a table, or "classification matrix," to portray the results. This will allow us to see when the errors occur most frequently.

Table 12 is the classification matrix for the Senate roll call data. Bardes's six scales correctly predicted the factional memberships for all but one of the Senators (Capehart) with "known" factional loyalties. This is 94.7% accuracy (sum of correct predictions, 18, divided by total predictions of "known" cases, 19). We can also see that the errors in this example are due to the incomplete separation of groups 1 and 4.

The bottom line of Table 12 also gives the classification distribution of the "unknown" cases. These are the Senators for whom Bardes was unable to determine factional positions on the basis of substantive evidence. Her chief purpose for using discriminant analysis was to classify these Senators on the basis of their voting records. She was then able to proceed with a substantive investigation of Senate support for various foreign aid alternatives.

The percentage of the "known" cases which are correctly classified is an additional measure of group differences. We can use it along with the overall Wilks's lambda and the canonical correlations to indicate the amount of discrimination contained in the variables. As a direct measure of predictive accuracy, this percentage is the most intuitive measure of discrimination. One should, however, judge the magnitude of this percentage in relation to the expected percentage of correct classifications if assignments were made randomly. If we have two groups, we can expect to get 50% of the predictions right by pure random assignment. With four groups, our expected accuracy is only 25%. Should the classification process yield only 60% correct predictions between the two groups, the improvement is rather small. With four groups, however, 60% correct prediction is a considerable improvement, because we would expect only 25% to be correct by chance. A proportional reduction in error statistic,

TABLE 12
Classification Matrix

Original Group	Predicted Group			
	1	2	3	4
1	8	0	0	1
2	0	2	0	0
3	0	0	5	0
4	0	0	0	3
Unknown	33	10	27	4

tau, which will give a standardized measure of improvement regardless of the number of groups, is:

$$\text{tau} = \frac{n_c - \sum_{i=1}^{g} p_i n_i}{n. - \sum_{i=1}^{g} p_i n_i} \qquad [17]$$

where n_c is the number of cases correctly classified and p_i is the prior probability of group membership. The term involving the summation is the number of cases that would be correctly classified on the basis of random assignment to groups in proportion to the prior probabilities. If the groups are to be treated equally, then all the prior probabilities are set to one divided by the number of groups. The maximum value for tau is 1.0, and it occurs when there are no errors in prediction. A value of zero indicates no improvement. Negative results are also possible, and they indicate no discrimination or a degenerate situation. Because n_c must be an integer, the numerator could become slightly negative due to chance when there are no group differences.

For Bardes's data, each group had a prior probability of .25. Consequntly, the summation used for tau is $(.25 \times 9) + (.25 \times 2) + (.25 \times 5) + (.25 \times 3) = 4.75$. With 18 correct predictions out of 19 total cases,

$$\text{tau} = \frac{18 - 4.75}{19 - 4.75} = \frac{13.25}{14.25} = .93.$$

This means that classification based on the discriminating variables made 93% fewer errors than would be expected by random assignment (i.e., 1 actual error versus 14.25 expected by chance).

Split-Sample Validation

As with any inferential technique based on sample data, the percent correct prediction and tau tend to overestimate the power of the classification procedure. This is because the validation is based on the same cases used to derive the classification functions. The equations utilize idiosyncratic sampling error to create classification functions which are more accurate for that particular sample than they would be for the full population.[24]

When the sample is large enough, we can validate the classification procedure by randomly splitting the sample into two subsets. One subset is used to derive the functions and the other is used only to test the classifications. Because each subset will tend to have different sampling errors, the test subset will give a better estimate of the ability to correctly predict the total population.

Statisticians tend to disagree on the appropriate sizes for the two subsets. Some recommend that they be equal, while others prefer more cases for one or the other subset. The most important consideration, however, is that the subset used to derive the functions be sufficiently large to insure stability of the coefficients or else the test will be flawed from the start.

We have seen in this chapter that various classification procedures allow us to predict the group membership of individual data cases. This is useful for the information it provides about (1) the specific data cases, (2) the differences between groups, and (3) the ability of the variables, as a set, to accurately discriminate among the groups. Our discussion so far has assumed that our set of discriminating variables is the optimal combination. I now turn to strategies for locating some subset of these variables which is more parsimonious and nearly as effective.

5. STEPWISE INCLUSION OF VARIABLES

Researchers often encounter situations in which they have several potential discriminating variables but they are uncertain whether all of them are valuable and necessary. This situation is frequently the result of substantive theories which are not strong enough to specify the precise list of discriminating variables. Consequently, the researchers collect data on variables which they merely "suspect" are good discriminators. Or perhaps the investigation is exploratory and the researchers are trying to discover useful discriminating variables.

In these situations, one or more of the variables may be poor discriminators, because the group means are not very different on those variables. Also, two or more of the variables may share the same discriminating information even though they are individually good discriminators. When some of these are employed in the analysis, the remainder are redundant. Although they may be good discriminators on their own, these redundant variables do not contribute to the analysis, because their *unique* contributions are insufficient. Unless there are strong theoretical reasons for keeping them, it is advisable to eliminate weak or redundant variables. Their presence only complicates the analysis and they may even increase the number of misclassifications.

One way to eliminate unnecessary variables is by using a stepwise procedure to select the most useful discriminating variables. A forward stepwise procedure begins by selecting the individual variable which provides the greatest univariate discrimination. The procedure then pairs this first variable with each of the remaining variables, one at a time, to locate the combination which produces the greatest discrimination. The variable which contributed to the best pair is selected. The procedure goes on to combine the first two with each of the remaining variables to form triplets. The best triplet determines the third variable to be entered. This procedure of selecting variables on the basis of the one which adds the most discrimination to those already selected continues until all possible variables have been selected or the remaining variables do not contribute a sufficient increment.

A stepwise procedure could also work in the backward direction in which all variables are initially considered to be "in" and the worst one is cast out at each step. Forward and backward selection can also be combined. Typically this involves a forward selection procedure with each step starting with a review of the variables previously selected. If any of these variables no longer makes a sufficient contribution to the discrimination, it is cast out although it remains eligible for reselection at a future step. The removal of previously selected variables is usually the result of shared discriminating information with other variables selected on intervening steps. At the time it was selected, this variable may have made a unique contribution. However, variables selected on subsequent steps may combine with one another or with variables selected earlier to duplicate the contribution of this variable. The variable is then redundant and a candidate for removal.

Stepwise procedures produce an optimal set of discriminating variables. This set may not be the best (maximal) combination. To secure a maximal solution, one would have to test all possible combinations (all possible pairs, all possible triplets, and so on). Such testing can be costly and time consuming. The stepwise procedure is a logical and efficient way to seek the best combination, but it cannot guarantee that the end product is indeed superior to all others.

The sequence in which variables are selected does not necessarily coincide with their relative importance. Because of intercorrelations (shared discriminating power), an important discriminator may be selected late or not at all, because its unique contributions are not as great as those of other variables.

Selection Criteria

Stepwise procedures must employ some measure of discrimination as the criterion for selection. Wilks's lambda is one such criterion, but there are alternatives which can be used to maximize various notions of group differences. In this section, I will review several of these alternative measures. Which one is "best" depends upon the research situation. The end result will often be the same regardless of the criterion used, but this is not always the case.

WILKS'S LAMBDA AND THE PARTIAL F RATIO

Wilks's lambda is a statistic which takes into consideration both the differences between groups and the cohesiveness or homogeneity within groups. By cohesiveness I mean the degree to which cases cluster near their group centroid. Thus, a variable which increases cohesiveness without changing the separation between the centroids may be selected over a variable which increases separation without changing the cohesiveness.

Because Wilks's lambda is an inverse statistic, we would select the variable which produced the *smallest* lambda for that step. As discussed earlier, we can convert lambda into an overall, multivariate F statistic for the test of group differences. If this F is used instead of lambda, we select on the *largest* F. Rather than using the overall F, we can employ the partial F, which is computed as the F-to-enter (see below). All three statistics yield the same results.

RAO'S V

Rao (1952: 257) built upon Mahalanobis's (1963) distance statistic to get a measure of total group separation. This generalized distance measure, known as Rao's V, applies to any number of groups. It measures the separation of group centroids and does not concern itself with cohesiveness within the groups. Thus, a variable selected on the basis of V may be decreasing within-group cohesion while it adds to the overall separation. The distances measured by V are from each group centroid to the grand centroid weighted by the group size. So V does not insure maximum separation between every *pair* of groups. (This is also true for Wilks's lambda.) The formula for V is:

$$V = (n. - g) \sum_{i=1}^{p'} \sum_{j=1}^{p'} a_{ij} \sum_{k=1}^{g} n_j (X_{ik.} - X_{i..}) (X_{jk.} - X_{j..}), \quad [18]$$

where p' is the number of variables entered (including the one being entered on the current step).

When there are a large number of cases, V has a sampling distribution approximately the same as chi-square with degrees of freedom equal to $p'(g - 1)$. In addition, the change in V due to the addition (or deletion) of variables also has a chi-square distribution with degrees of freedom equal to $(g - 1)$ times the number of variables added (deleted) at that step. We can use this property to test the statistical significance of the change in overall separation. If the change is not significant, we would not want to include the variable. As we add variables, the change in V can be negative. This indicates that the selected variable caused a decrease in overall separation of the centroids.

MAHALANOBIS SQUARED DISTANCE
BETWEEN CLOSEST GROUPS

Rather than concentrating on total group separation, we may want to pick the variable which generates the greatest separation for the pair of groups which are closest at that step. This will tend to force all the groups to be separated. We can choose among three statistics to measure this separation, and all of them are based on the Mahalanobis squared distance between the pairs of group centroids.

Of course, one of these statistics is D^2 itself. This is a direct, intuitive measure which gives equal weight to each pair of groups.

BETWEEN-GROUPS F

An F statistic for the differences between two groups is given by the following formula:

$$F = \frac{(n. - g - p' + 1) \, n_i n_j}{p' (n. - g) (n_i + n_j)} \, D^2(G_i | G_j). \quad [19]$$

This differs from a test based only on the squared distance, because it considers the *sample* size of the groups. Comparisons between small groups will be given less weight than comparisons between large groups. So this criterion will tend to maximize differences between pairs containing larger groups.

MINIMIZING RESIDUAL VARIANCE

A fifth possible criterion aims at minimizing the residual variance between groups. The formula is:

$$R = \sum_{i=1}^{g-1} \sum_{j=i+1}^{g} \frac{4}{4 + D^2(G_i \mid G_j)}. \qquad [20]$$

Each term in the summation is an estimate of one minus the square of the multiple correlation between the set of discriminating variables being considered and a dummy variable which identifies the corresponding pair of groups. This is the residual variance, because each term is the proportion of variation in the dummy variable *not* explained by the discriminating variables. Sometimes R is divided by the number of pairs, $g(g-1)/2$, to yield the average residual variance between groups, but that does not affect the choice of the variable to be selected. Also, one can employ weights for each pair if some pairs are to be given greater importance over others (see Dixon, 1973: 243).

By considering all the pairs at once, R tends to promote an equal separation of the groups. This differs slightly from the first two criteria in which two groups could be left close to one another if large gains are made in separating other groups or improving within-group cohesion. It also differs from the third and fourth criteria in which each step only looks at the closest pair.

Minimum Conditions for Selection

Most stepwise selection programs require a variable to pass certain minimum conditions before it is tested on the selection criterion. These conditions are a tolerance test to assure computational accuracy and a partial F statistic to assure that the increased discrimination exceeds some level determined by the user.[25] Some programs also check the list of variables already entered to determine if any should be deleted.

TOLERANCE

The tolerance test is designed to preserve computational accuracy. The tolerance for a variable not yet selected is one minus the squared multiple correlation between that variable and all variables already entered, when the correlations are based on the within-groups correlation matrix. If the variable being tested is a linear combination (or nearly a linear combination) of one or more of the variables already entered, its tolerance will be zero (or near zero). A variable with a small tolerance (say less than .001) is likely to cause inaccuracies in computing the inverse of the final W matrix because of the rapid accumulation of rounding errors. In addition to the computational problems, one would not want to include a variable which is a linear combination of others already included, because it has no unique information to contribute.

F-TO-ENTER

The F-to-enter is a partial multivariate F statistic which tests the additional discrimination introduced by the variable being considered after taking into account the discrimination achieved by the other variables already entered (Dixon, 1973: 241). If this F is small, we do not want to select that variable, because it is not adding enough to the overall discrimination. We can also use this F statistic as a test of significance to see if the increment is statistically significant. The degrees of freedom are (g − 1) and (n. − p′ − g + 1). A variable must pass the tolerance and F-to-enter tests before it is tested on the entry criterion.

F-TO-REMOVE

The F-to-remove is also a partial multivariate F statistic, but it tests the significance of the decrease in discrimination should that variable be removed from the list of variables already selected. Its degrees of freedom are (g − 1) and (n. − p′ − g). This test is performed at the beginning of each step to see if there are any variables which no longer make a sufficiently large unique contribution to discrimination. A variable that was a good choice on an earlier step may no longer be valuable, because variables entered later duplicate its contribution.

On the final step, the F-to-remove statistic can be used to obtain the rank order of the unique discriminating power carried by each of the selected variables. The variable with the largest F-to-remove makes the greatest contribution to overall discrimination above and beyond the contributions already made by the other variables. The variable with the second largest F-to-remove is the second most important, and so forth. This is not necessarily the same ranking that would be obtained from a univariate F, because the univariate F measures the variable's total discriminating power without considering how much might be shared by other variables.

A Stepwise Example

To see how the stepwise procedure works in practice, let us apply this technique to Bardes's Senate roll call data. When the Mahalanobis squared distance between the closest groups is used as the entry criterion, we obtain the results reported in Table 13.

On the first step, the tolerance is always 1.0, because no variables have been entered yet, and the F-to-enter corresponds to the univariate F statistic for the same reason. The fourth column gives the values for D^2 among which we are to select the largest. That value, .492, is produced by CUTASIAN when comparing group 1 to group 4. Note that the closest pair for CUTASIAN may not be the closest pair for any of the other variables (with four groups there are six pairs to be considered). Our choice of the squared distance statistic as the entry criterion was based on the presumption we want to emphasize separation between the closest groups as it is affected by the variable being examined. There was no special reason for using this criterion other than to illustrate the workings of the stepwise method. In this instance, CUTASIAN is an obvious choice, because both the squared distance and F-to-enter values are much larger than for any of the other variables. Note, however, that on this step the squared distance for ANTINEUT is more than 10 times the value for CUTAID even though they have nearly equal values for F-to-enter.

At step 2, the procedure has recomputed all the relevant statistics taking into account that CUTASIAN has already entered. Now, the tolerance will almost certainly be less than one, because it represents one minus the squared correlation between CUTASIAN and the respective variable. The F-to-enter is the partial F for the discrimination added by the respective variable after CUTASIAN has created as much discrimination as possible. And the squared distance is the smallest value produced over all six pairs of groups by CUTASIAN and the given variable working together. Here, ANTINEUT produces the largest of these smallest values.

The process is repeated at step 3. Because we are using the squared distances as the entry criterion, RESTRICT is the next to enter. However,

TABLE 13

Entry Statistics for Stepwise Selection, by Step

	Variable	Tolerance	F-to-enter	Squared Distance	Between Groups
AT STEP 1					
	CUTAID	1.000	2.955	.018	3 and 4
	RESTRICT	1.000	.943	.004	1 and 3
	CUTASIAN	1.000	11.915	.492*	1 and 4
	MIXED	1.000	2.628	.038	3 and 4
	ANTIYUGO	1.000	4.168	.019	2 and 3
	ANTINEUT	1.000	2.900	.194	3 and 4
AT STEP 2					
	CUTAID	.521	.748	.820	1 and 4
	RESTRICT	.684	3.418	.495	1 and 4
	MIXED	.305	7.981	3.014	1 and 4
	ANTIYUGO	.851	2.898	3.370	3 and 4
	ANTINEUT	.383	8.502	3.801*	1 and 4
AT STEP 3					
	CUTAID	.507	.700	4.590	1 and 4
	RESTRICT	.446	1.228	5.405*	1 and 4
	MIXED	.282	1.496	5.094	1 and 4
	ANTIYUGO	.546	1.376	4.730	1 and 4
AT STEP 4					
	CUTAID	.486	.701	5.823	1 and 4
	MIXED	.282	1.378	6.743	1 and 4
	ANTIYUGO	.488	1.887	7.519*	1 and 4
AT STEP 5					
	CUTAID	.407	1.234	7.523	1 and 4
	MIXED	.282	1.236	8.186*	1 and 4
AT STEP 6					
	CUTAID	.330	.672	9.043*	1 and 4

*Denotes variable selected at that step as determined by the Mahalanobis distance squared between the two closest groups.

if we had used Wilks's lambda as the entry criterion, as measured indirectly by the F-to-enter, we would have entered MIXED instead. The disagreement is due to the different aspects of discrimination that each possible criterion emphasizes.

The remaining steps proceed in a similar fashion until all the variables have been entered. At step 6, CUTAID has an F-to-enter value which is rather low and we might choose to prevent it from entering the analysis.

Also at step 6, the F-to-remove for ANTINEUT has fallen to .996. Some researchers would feel this is small enough to justify the removal of ANTINEUT. If the program had done this, step 6 would have shown the removal of ANTINEUT. Then the stepwise procedure would have gone to step 7 where it would have considered entering CUTAID and ANTINEUT. Because the procedure would have found that neither of these variables has a sufficiently high F-to-enter, the entry process would have halted and the remaining discriminant analysis and classification would have used only the other four variables.

This example was structured to allow all the variables to enter, because Bardes's original research used all six variables. Indeed, she had substantive reasons for using all the variables, so she did not utilize the stepwise procedure at all. If one is going to employ all of the variables anyway, there is very little benefit to pursuing a stepwise analysis. The rationale for this technique is to find variables to eliminate, because their unique contributions are small. On the basis of Table 13, one could even argue that the selection of variables should have stopped at the end of step 2, because none of the F's are significant at step 3. We could have stopped after step 2 and proceeded with the classification. If the number of errors made with only those two variables (CUTASIAN and ANTINEUT) is less or nearly the same as when all six variables are used, we would be justified in eliminating the other four. In some situations, the use of more variables actually leads to less accurate classifications.

The purpose of stepwise selection is to locate a more parsimonious subset of variables which can discriminate nearly as well as, if not better than, the full set. This chapter has outlined strategies for pursuing such a goal. In addition to deciding whether the research situation warrants the use of stepwise selection, the researcher may need to face several other practical considerations, such as violations of assumptions and the consequences of missing data. The concluding chapter deals with these annoying, but crucial problems.

6. CONCLUDING REMARKS

Violation of Assumptions

At several points I have touched on the problems which arise when the data do not satisfy all of the mathematical assumptions of discriminant analysis. The most difficult assumptions to meet are the requirements for a multivariate normal distribution on the discriminating variables and equal group covariance matrices. Several authors (see in particular Lachenbruch, 1975) have shown that discriminant analysis is a rather robust technique which can tolerate some deviation from these assumptions. In addition, not all of the aspects of discriminant analysis require these assumptions.

The assumption of a multivariate normal distribution is important for tests of significance. In such tests we are comparing a statistic computed from a sample to a theoretical probability distribution for that statistic. We can compute a theoretical distribution by making some convenient mathematical assumptions, such as requiring that the population have a multivariate normal distribution. If our population of interest does not satisfy this requirement, the true sampling distribution for our statistic will be somewhat different from our theoretically derived distribution. The differences between the two distributions may be very small or very large, depending on the degree of deviation from the assumption. Lachenbruch (1975) has shown that discriminant analysis is not particularly sensitive to minor violations of the normality assumption. The consequence is some reduction in efficiency and accuracy.

The normality assumption is also important for classification based on the probability of group membership. These probabilities are calculated from the chi-square distribution which is appropriate only when the discriminating variables have a multivariate normal distribution. When they do not meet this assumption, the calculated probabilities will be inaccurate. It may turn out, for example, that the probabilities for some groups will be exaggerated while the probabilities for other groups will be underestimated. Consequently, this procedure will not be optimal, in the sense of minimizing the number of misclassifications.

When the group covariance matrices are not equal, we tend to get distortions in the canonical discriminant functions and the classification equations. One source of error is in computing the within-groups covariance matrix (or the related W matrix). The within-covariance matrix is meant to be an estimate of the common (equal) group covariance matrices in the population based on the several group samples. If the population matrices are not equal, the W matrix can still be calculated, but it does not properly fulfill its function of simplifying various formulas. Consequently, the canonical discriminant functions may not provide maximum separation among the groups, and the probabilities of group membership will be distorted. While there do not seem to be any procedures for improving the canonical discriminant functions, several of the texts mentioned earlier suggest using the individual group covariance matrices for computing the probability of group membership (this is called "quadratic discrimination").

Discriminant analysis can be performed when the assumptions of multivariate normal distributions and equal group covariance matrices are not satisfied. The problem comes in using the results. What do they mean? And how much error can be tolerated? Several advanced texts suggest alternative procedures, but these often yield only minimal improvement, because the original deviation is not severe. Of course, we are rarely in a position to know how much error has been introduced by our particular violation of assumptions. We may, however, get some guidance from certain statistics which do not rely on these assumptions.

In determining the importance and minimum number of canonical discriminant functions, we do not have to rely on Wilks's lambda or its associated chi-square test of significance. Instead, we can examine the canonical correlation and relative percentage as explained in Chapter 2. If either of these values is small we would not have much interest in the function even if it were statistically significant. Our greatest interest in tests of significance occurs when the samples are small. Thus, with small samples we should be more careful about satisfying assumptions. With large samples, however, we can ignore the tests of significance or interpret them "conservatively" when our data violate the assumptions.

For classification purposes, the accuracy of the prediction is most important for borderline cases. If a particular case has a .90 probability of belonging to group 1 and only a .10 probability of belonging to group 2, we do not have to worry about small inaccuracies due to the violation of assumptions. Although the specific probability of group membership may be wrong, our decision to assign the case to group 1 would be correct unless there was a major error in the calculation of the probabilities. On the other hand, if the case had probabilities of .51 for group 1 and .49 for group 2, we would want to be very cautious about our decision. Here, minor errors due to the violation of assumptions could easily cause an incorrect classification.

For the researcher whose main interest is in a mathematical model which can predict well or serve as a reasonable description of the real world, the best guide is the percentage of correct classifications. If this percentage is high, the violation of assumptions was not very harmful. Efforts to improve the data or use alternative formulas can give only marginal improvements. When the percentage of correct classifications is low, however, we cannot tell whether this is due to violating the assumptions or using weak discriminating variables.

Other Problems

Several other problems, which are beyond the scope of this paper, could plague the user of discriminant analysis. These include large amounts of missing data, highly correlated variables, a variable with zero standard deviations within one or more groups, grossly different group sizes, and outliers. Although I will not discuss these problems, the reader should be aware that such pathologies can have a negative effect upon the accuracy and interpretation of a discriminant analysis.

In Conclusion

Although this chapter has focused on some of the problems and difficulties in using discriminant analysis, no one should be discouraged by them. In practical research situations, we must often contend with data that do not conform nicely to the assumptions of our statistical technique. By being familiar with the requirements of the model, we will know when they are being violated, when to apply corrective measures, and when the technique is inappropriate for the given research situation.

This paper has been intended as a thorough introduction to discriminant analysis. By now, the reader should be aware that this includes a series of statistical procedures for (1) studying the multivariate differences between two or more groups (which we have called the "interpretation" activity) and (2) using several variables to predict group membership of individual cases (called "classification"). The mathematical model generally assumes that the variables are interval level with a multivariate normal distribution. I have also restricted this discussion to linear discriminant analysis, which usually requires equal-group covariance matrices. With this background a researcher can make considerable use of the discriminant analysis routines in the standard computer programs, such as SPSS, BMD, and SAS. The reader who wants to learn more about any of the features of discriminant analysis can pursue them in the more advanced texts cited in the list of references.

NOTES

1. Stevens (1946, 1951) defined four levels of measurement: nominal, ordinal, interval, and ratio. For an interval level measure, the important distinction is that the measurement scheme produces an assignment of numbers such that the real magnitude of the distance between any pair of consecutive integers on the scale is equal to the distance between any other pair of consecutive integers. Ideally, the measurement scheme will be continuous, but this is not absolutely necessary. The measurement must be at least interval level, because discriminant analysis requires the computation of means, variances, and covariances. For further details on levels of measurement, see Blalock (1979: 15-19), Nie et al. (1975: 4-6), or almost any introductory statistics text.

2. The covariance between two variables is a measure of how much they vary together. It is somewhat like a correlation coefficient, but it has not been standardized for the different scale magnitudes on the variables. Consequently, a covariance can take on any value and is not limited to the range of -1.0 through $+1.0$. We often arrange covariances (and other statistics) into a special table called a "matrix." The matrix has one row and one column for each variable. The intersection of a row and column contains the covariance for the corresponding pair of variables. The diagonal going from the upper-left corner to the lower-right corner contains variances, because the covariance of a variable with itself is the same as its variance. When data are divided into groups, we can compute a covariance matrix for each group by using only the cases from that group. For two covariance matrices to be equal (or identical), the entries in each cell on one matrix must be equal to the corresponding entries on the other matrix. Most introductory statistics texts discuss the concepts of variance and covariance and provide formulas. In particular, see Blalock (1979: 80 and 392).

3. Many of the tables presented here were adapted from Bardes (1975: Chapter 5). When necessary, additional details were obtained by rerunning the original data, which Bardes kindly supplied. The numeric values Bardes reported for the coefficients, centroids, and discriminant scores differ from those reported here due to a change in the way the discriminant functions were standardized. This change does not affect the substantive interpretations or the classification results. The computer program used was the SPSS DISCRIMINANT routine in the IBM 360/370 Release 8.0.

4. One could perform a one-way analysis of variance on each variable to see if the overall group differences are statistically significant (see Iversen and Norpoth, 1976, or most intro-

ductory statistics texts). Variables which do not show signficant group differences at the univariate level usually do poorly in a discriminant analysis. The reader should note that tests of significance are not applicable (in a strict interpretation of statistical theory) to Bardes's data, because she is studying a population rather than a sample.

5. A matrix is a two-dimensional array of numbers. By using a single symbol for the matrix, we can easily talk about many related numbers that are to be treated in a similar fashion. Each number within a matrix is called an element. The usual symbol for the element is the lowercase letter with two subscripts, where the first denotes the row location and the second denotes the column location. Thus, t_{ij} is one of the numbers from matrix T, it can be found at the intersection of row i and column j. When $i = j$ in a square matrix, we say it is on the diagonal running from the upper left to the lower right. A matrix is square when the number of rows equals the number of columns. When a matrix is symmetric the upper-right triangle is a reflection of the lower-left triangle—that is, $t_{ij} = t_{ji}$.

6. See Cooley and Lohnes (1971: Chapter 9) or a similar text for more details on solving the general eigenvalue problem and standardizing the discriminant function. Cooley and Lohnes suggest standardizing on the T matrix rather than W. This is generally legitimate, although the meaning of the discriminant scores is changed somewhat. As explained in the text, W produces scores which represent standard deviation units *within the groups*. T yields scores which are standard deviation units for the *total space* and are, therefore, smaller numbers. The difference is only the frame of reference one wishes to use. The choice does not affect the substantive interpretations or the classification results. However, the value for the statistic $Pr(X|G_k)$, see Chapter 4, can be computed correctly only when W is used. The examples in this text were based on standardization by W, which is the more common procedure.

7. When the discriminant function coefficients have been standardized according to the W matrix, the most common method, a score of 1.0 denotes one standard deviation *within a group*. Thus, if we were to take the cases for any one group and compute their standard deviation on the function from *that group's mean*, the resulting value would be (approximately) 1.0. This assumes, of course, that the group covariance matrices are equal and accurately represented by the within-groups covariance matrix. If, instead, we were to compute the standard deviation for *all* the cases relative to the *grand* mean, the resulting value would be greater than one (unless the group centroids are identical). The idea is that the groups (rather than the total system) define the basic units on which all distances are calculated. As noted earlier, one could standardize on the T matrix, in which instance the standard deviation for all cases from the grand mean will be 1.0. This is legitimate and merely implies a shift in one's frame of reference.

8. Note that the direction of a function is arbitrary. By changing the signs for all the coefficients on a given function, one merely reverses the direction of the axis. Either direction is just as "good" as the other. The only rationale for preferring one direction over the other would be a situation in which certain cases intuitively "belong" at a particular end. For example, if the roll call votes resulted in a liberal-conservative continuum, it is convention to place the liberals on the left (negative) side.

9. Note that the raw data values are the same for each function. This is because a data case has only one position on each variable, and all of the variables must be used in computing each discriminant score.

10. By standard form, or Z scores, I mean that the values on a given variable have been adjusted so that they have a mean of zero and a standard deviation of one. We achieve this by subtracting the grand mean of the variable from each individual value and dividing the results by the standard deviation.

11. For readers who are familiar with multiple regression, the interpretation of unstandardized and standardized discriminant coefficients is analogous to the interpretation

of regular and standardized multiple regression coefficients. Also, in this example the standard deviations for the six scales are nearly equal. Consequently, the relative magnitude of the coefficients changes only slightly when they are standardized. This is not always the case when the standard deviations are of differing magnitudes.

12. Again, one must take care to standardize properly. If the W matrix has been used to standardize the coefficients, then the discriminating variables must be standardized according to the grand mean and the *within-groups* standard deviation. When T has been used, standardize the variables by the grand mean and the *total* standard deviation. In practice, we normally use the raw scores with the unstandardized discriminant function coefficients to compute the discriminant scores. The standardized coefficients are used only for making substantive interpretations.

13. Total structure coefficients can be obtained in two ways. One is to have a computer program compute the discriminant score for each function using Equation 1 and then employ a Pearson correlation program to compute the correlations between the functions and the variables. Alternatively, we can compute the standardized canonical discriminant function coefficients based on the T matrix from the following formula:

$$c_{kj}^* = \frac{v_{kj} \sqrt{t_{kk}}}{\sqrt{\sum_{i=1}^{p} \sum_{m=1}^{p} v_{ij} v_{mj} t_{im}}} \qquad [21]$$

where c_{kj}^* is the function coefficient for function j and variable k. (The denominator of this equation is a constant and needs to be evaluated only once.) The total structure coefficients are obtained from:

$$s_{ij} = \sum_{k=1}^{p} r_{ik} c_{kj}^* = \sum_{k=1}^{p} \frac{t_{ik} c_{kj}^*}{\sqrt{t_{ii} t_{kk}}} \qquad [22]$$

where s_{ij} is the total structure coefficient (correlation) for variable i and function j and r_{ik} is the total correlation between variables i and k.

14. These results assume a positive correlation between the pair of variables. If the correlation is negative, the opposite effect can occur. In practice there are multiple correlations which make the interpretation of the standardized coefficients even more difficult.

15. Substantive significance is the ability of a research finding to have meaning in explaining the phenomenon under investigation.

16. Many statistics texts use the term *canonical variate* to refer to what we have been calling the "canonical discriminant function." They also use "discriminant function" to denote what we will call a "classification function" in Chapter 4. Other authors, such as Cooley and Lohnes (1971), apply the term *discriminant function* to the "canonical discriminant function." To avoid this terminological confusion, we will use "canonical discriminant function" and "classification function."

17. The reader should note that the canonical correlations in Table 9 are influenced by the small number of cases (19). Larger samples (over 1000 cases or so) have greater difficulty yielding high correlations, because they are typically more heterogeneous.

18. By "population data" I mean that the data cases under study exhaust the population: They are not a sample.

19. Readers who are not familiar with the concept of statistical significance should consult Henkel (1976) or an introductory statistics text which deals with inferential statistics. An important point to keep in mind is that statistical significance and substantive significance are very different concepts. Statistical significance is primarily a test of whether the sample is sufficiently large for one to be confident that the statistic in question is actually different from the hypothesized value (usually zero or "no difference"). With a large sample, a statistic could be statistically significant while lacking substantive significance (for example, a small canonical correlation).

20. Chi-square and F are theoretical probability distributions which measure the probability that a difference in group means observed in the sample is due to chance sampling variation when, in fact, there is no difference in the population. Each of these distributions has a different shape depending on the "degrees of freedom" associated with the particular problem. One must know the degrees of freedom before consulting a table to determine the probability level associated with the computed chi-square or F value.

21. The cases used in this example are not a simple random sample. Consequently, the test of significance does not apply here under a strict interpretation of the underlying assumptions. For the sake of the continuity of the example, the test will be used here anyway.

22. Some "discriminant analysis" programs (such as BMD05M and the routine in SAS76) perform only classification and do not compute the canonical discriminant functions.

23. The inverse of a (square) matrix is another matrix which has the property that when the two are multiplied together the result is a matrix with ones along the major diagonal and zeroes elsewhere. For further information on matrix inverses and how to calculate them, see an advanced statistics text which employs matrix algebra, such as Cooley and Lohnes (1971).

24. See Lachenbruch (1975: 29-36) for a discussion of this problem and suggestions for alternative error rates.

25. The formulas for the tolerance, F-to-enter, and F-to-remove statistics are rather complicated and will not be given here. The interested reader can consult Norusis (1979: 73-74).

REFERENCES

ANDERSON, T. W. (1958) An Introduction to Multivariate Statistical Analysis. New York: John Wiley.

BARDES, B. A. (1976) "Senatorial support for foreign policy: a comparison of alternative explanations." Presented at the meeting of the Midwest Political Science Association, Chicago, April 29-May 1.

——— (1975) "Senatorial realignment on foreign aid, 1953-1972: a discriminant analysis of inter-party factions." Ph.D. dissertation, University of Cincinnati.

BARR, A. J., J. H. GOODNIGHT, J. P. SALL, and J. T. HELWIG (1976) A Users's Guide to SAS-76. Raleigh, NC: Sparks Press.

BLALOCK, H. M., Jr. (1979) Social Statistics. New York: McGraw-Hill.

COOLEY, W. W. and P. R. LOHNES (1971) Multivariate Data Analysis. New York: John Wiley.

DIXON, W. J. [ed.] (1973) BMD: Biomedical Programs. Berkeley: University of California Press.

EISENSTEIN, J. and H. JACOB (1977) Felony Justice. Boston: Little, Brown.

FISHER, R. A. (1936) "The use of multiple measurements in taxonomic problems." Annals of Eugenics 7: 179-188.

HENKEL, R. E. (1976) Tests of Significance. Sage University Paper series on Quantitative Applications in the Social Sciences, 07-004. Beverly Hills and London: Sage Publications.

HEYCK, T. W. and W. R. KLECKA (1973) "British radical M.P.'s, 1874-1895: new evidence from discriminant analysis." Journal of Interdisciplinary History 4 (Autumn): 161-184.

IVERSEN, G. R. and H. NORPOTH (1976) Analysis of Variance. Sage University Paper series on Quantitative Applications in the Social Sciences, 07-001. Beverly Hills and London: Sage Publications.

KENDALL, M. G. (1968) A Course in Multivariate Analysis. New York: Hafner.

KLECKA, C. O. (1974) "The measurement of children's masculinity and femininity." Ph.D. dissertation, Northwestern University.

KLECKA, W. R. (1975) "Discriminant analysis," pp. 434-467 in N. Nie et al. SPSS: Statistical Package for the Social Sciences. New York: McGraw-Hill.

——— (1973) "The clientele of Australian parties: new perspectives through discriminant analysis." Politics 7: 301-308.

KORNBERG, A. and R. C. FRASURE (1971) "Policy differences in British parliamentary parties." American Political Science Review 65: 694-703.

LACHENBRUCH, P. A. (1975) Discriminant Analysis. New York: Hafner.

LEVINE, M. S. (1977) Canonical Analysis and Factor Comparison. Sage University Paper series on Quantitative Applications in the Social Sciences, 07-006. Beverly Hills and London: Sage Publications.

MAHALANOBIS, P. C. (1963) "On the generalized distance in statistics." Proceedings of the National Institute of Science, India 12: 49-55.

MORRISON, D. G. (1974) "Discriminant analysis," pp. 2.442-2.457 in R. Ferber (ed.), Handbook of Marketing Research. New York: John Wiley.

——— (1969) "On the interpretation of discriminant analysis." Journal of Marketing Research 6: 156-163.

NIE, N. H., C. H. HULL, J. G. JENKINS, K. STEINBRENNER, and D. H. BENT (1975) SPSS: Statistical Package for the Social Sciences. New York: McGraw-Hill.

NORUSIS, M. J. (1979) SPSS Statistical Algorithms: Release 8.0. Chicago: SPSS, Inc.

OVERALL, J. E. and C. J. KLETT (1972) Applied Multivariate Analysis. New York: McGraw-Hill.

RAO, C. R. (1965) Linear Statistical Inference and Its Applications. New York: John Wiley.

——— (1952) Advanced Statistical Methods in Biometric Research. New York: John Wiley.

STEVENS, S. S. (1951) "Mathematics, measurement, and psychophysics," pp. 1-49 in S. S. Stevens (ed.), The Handbook of Experimental Psychology. New York: John Wiley.

——— (1946) "On the theory of scales of measurement." Science 103: 677-680.

TATSUOKA, M. M. (1971) Multivariate Analysis. New York: John Wiley.

——— and D. V. TIEDEMAN (1954) "Discriminant analysis." Review of Educational Research 24: 402-420.

VAN DE GEER, J. P. (1971) Introduction to Multivariate Analysis for the Social Sciences. San Francisco: W. H. Freeman.

VELDMAN, D. J. (1967) Fortran Programming for the Behavioral Sciences. New York: Holt, Rinehart & Winston.

WILLIAM R. KLECKA is Associate Professor of Political Science at the University of Cincinnati. His numerous articles deal with social science research methods, political behavior, and crime victimization. He has coauthored several books, including SPSS Primer *(1975 with Nie and Hull),* Random Digit Dialing *(1976 with Tuchfarber), and* Fear of Crime *(1977 with Skogan).*